Vulnerable Adults and Community Care

Post-qualifying Social Work Practice – other titles in the series

Advanced Social Work with Children and Families	ISBN 978 1 84445 363 4
Child Care Social Work	ISBN 978 1 84445 180 7
Critical Thinking for Social Work (2nd Edition)	ISBN 978 1 84445 157 9
Effective Leadership, Management and Supervision in Health and Social Care	ISBN 978 1 84445 181 4
Evidence-based Policy and Practice in Mental Health Social Work	ISBN 978 1 84445 149 4
Law and the Social Work Practitioner (2nd Edition)	ISBN 978 1 84445 264 4
Practice Education in Social Work	ISBN 978 1 84445 105 0
The Practice Educator's Handbook	ISBN 978 0 85725 094 0
Proactive Management in Social Work Practice	ISBN 978 1 84445 289 7
Professional Decision Making in Social Work	ISBN 978 1 84445 359 7
The Approved Mental Health Professional's Guide to Mental Health Law (2nd Edition)	ISBN 978 1 84445 115 9
The Approved Social Worker's Guide to Psychiatry and Medication (2nd Edition)	ISBN 978 1 84445 304 7
The Mental Capacity Act 2005: A Guide for Practice (2nd Edition)	ISBN 978 1 84445 294 1
Values and Ethics in Mental Health Practice	ISBN 978 1 84445 375 7

To order, please contact our distributor: BEBC Distribution, Albion Close, Parkstone, Poole BH12 3LL. Telephone: 0845 230 9000, email: **learningmatters@ bebc.co.uk**. You can also find more information on each of these titles and our other learning resources at **www.learningmatters.co.uk**.

Vulnerable Adults and Community Care

Second Edition

Edited by

KEITH BROWN

Series Editor: Keith Brown

LearningMatters

First published in 2010 by Learning Matters Ltd.

© Keith Brown

British Library Cataloguing in Publication Data
A CIP record for this book is available from the British Library.

ISBN: 978 1 84445 362 7

Cover and text design by Code 5 Design Ltd
Project management by Deer Park Productions
Typeset by Pantek Arts Ltd, Maidstone, Kent
Printed and bound in Great Britain by Bell & Bain Ltd, Glasgow

Learning Matters Ltd
20 Cathedral Yard
Exeter EX1 1HB
Tel: 01392 215560
info@learningmatters.co.uk
www.learningmatters.co.uk

5/15/12

Contents

About the Authors

Professor Keith Brown

Keith Brown holds professional qualifications in nursing, social work, and teaching and academic qualifications in nursing, social work and management. He has worked in education and training for more than 15 years, working for universities and council social work departments. Currently, Keith is the Head of the Centre for Post Qualifying Social Work at Bournemouth University. The centre was recently recognised with the National Prize at the 2005 National Training Awards and, at the same ceremony, Keith was awarded the Linda Ammon Memorial Prize sponsored by the Department for Education and Skills, given to the person who has made the greatest contribution to education and training in the UK. Keith regularly speaks at national and international conferences. He has also published in national and international journals.

Dr Lee-Ann Fenge

Prior to joining Bournemouth University as a lecturer in 1995, Lee-Ann worked in a number of settings in adult social services in both Dorset and London. Her particular interests are in practice with older people, and she is currently engaged in a number of research projects. This includes a three-year New Dynamics of Ageing project exploring rurality, ageing and sexuality, and a project exploring the impact of the recession on older people. She has a particular interest in participatory methodologies and engaging with the voices of marginalised groups

Michael Lyne

Michael joined Bournemouth University as a lecturer in mental health social work in 2009. Prior to this he was employed in a post joint-funded by a local authority and PCT in the south of England where he was responsible for the implementation and correct use of mental health legislation.

Registered as both a social worker and mental nurse, Michael has a unique insight into the issues faced by practitioners from both health and social care.

Michael's current interests are in capacity and consent to treatment, deprivation of liberty, substituted decision-making for incapacitated individuals and end-of-life care.

Eileen Qubain

Eileen began her career as a residential social worker, and after training at Cardiff, worked as a hospital social worker for nine years. Eileen now works in a team for older people and feels privileged to work alongside people in crisis. She also feels fortunate to have wonderful colleagues to work with.

Jonathan Monk

Jonathan is a registered social worker and currently works for Worcestershire County Council as the Joint Commissioning Manager for Learning Disability Services. In this role he is required to plan and design the services to meet the needs of people with learning disabilities. Prior to that, he was involved in developing and promoting self-directed support in the county. He has worked in a number of frontline services, including community adult disability teams.

Chris Willets

Chris is a senior lecturer in learning disabilities at Bournemouth University where he is involved in pre- and post-qualifying education for social workers, and other health and social care professionals. He also has a range of relevant experience working with children and adults with a learning difficulty in a range of care settings.

Linda Naylor

Linda Naylor is an independent trainer delivering mainly child and adult protection training for a variety of organisations. She worked as a social worker for 16 years, then as a local authority training officer specialising in adult protection. She was a senior lecturer at Bournemouth University before becoming self-employed. Her training and consultancy in adult protection means she has an overview of the development of this key area of work across the South of England.

Foreword to the Post-qualifying Social Work Practice series

All the texts in the Post-qualifying Social Work Practice Series have been written by people with a passion for excellence in social work practice. They are primarily written for social workers who are undertaking post-qualifying social work awards, but will also be useful to any social worker who wants to consider up-to-date social work practice issues.

The books in the series are also of value to social work students as they are written to inform, inspire and develop social work practice.

All the authors have a connection with the Centre for Post Qualifying Social Work, and as a Centre we are all committed to raising the profile of the social work profession. We trust you find this text of real value to your social work practice, and that this in turn has a real impact on the service that users and carers receive.

Introduction

This second edition has been updated with the inclusion of two new chapters – Chapter 3, The Mental Capacity Act 2005, and Chapter 9, People with learning difficulties – Issues of vulnerability. The other chapters in this book have been updated to reflect the ongoing changes in the field.

The primary aim of the book, however, remains to support candidates who wish to undertake a Post Qualifying Social Work Award in the field of community care and working with vulnerable adults though it is a valuable resource to all working with these client groups.

All the authors have a connection with the Centre for Post Qualifying Social Work and their commitment and dedication to seeing that the best possible social work practice is delivered is very evident. I know that I can state on behalf of all the contributors that it is our collective desire that this text inspires you, the reader, to reflect on your professional practice and to work in a way that ensures that the vulnerable members of our society are supported and protected to the highest standard possible.

Professor Keith Brown
Head of Post Qualifying Social Work

4th Floor
Royal London House
Christchurch Road
Bournemouth
Dorset BH1 3LT

Tel: 01202 964765
Email: **pqsw@bournemouth.ac.uk**

Chapter 1

Welfare policy: Context of community care

Professor Keith Brown

Introduction

This first chapter aims to consider and analyse British welfare policy and its recent developments and its impact on the community care agenda. Although it is in essence a social policy analysis, it is written to provide a clear background to the policy context within which social workers currently deliver community care. The philosophical areas of welfare capitalism and free-market thinking are considered in order to give a background to the current situation that social workers find themselves working within.

Social workers as professionals regulated by the General Social Care Council are required to abide by a set of professional standards which at their heart rightly have the needs of service users and carers. Yet the vast majority of social workers work for social work agencies (usually local authority social service departments) which have great budgeting pressures on them.

The central government pressure to keep down the cost of the council tax (Community Charge) is at odds with ever-increasing pressure for more and better-quality services, particularly for vulnerable adults. Thus councils are forced to prioritise (another word for 'ration') their service in order to stay within budget and this puts a pressure on the social worker. Here the social worker is under pressure as the resources the client might need may be simply too expensive. Also, there is the strange pressure which says 'please do not be effective in finding new clients who want help as we cannot afford to meet their needs'. In other words, in financial terms, it is better to employ social workers whose skills and abilities are in preventing new clients from wanting, seeking or finding help.

This chapter looks at the background to this dilemma and the developments of welfare policy which underpin the delivery of social work in the UK.

Welfare capitalism

Introduction

The aim of this section of the chapter is to provide a general sketch of a welfare perspective usually referred to as 'welfare capitalism'. (It has also been called 'collectivism', 'the post-war consensus', 'Butskellism' (Butler/Atshill) and the 'Keynesian welfare state').

Welfare capitalism dominated British governments' economic and welfare conceptions in the post-war years between 1945 and 1977, and it currently forms an important basis of opposition thinking. In terms of other societies, welfare capitalism forms an important ideological base for the economics and politics of: Australia, Austria, Canada, Finland and Sweden, and looks to be the conception of capitalism that many of the Eastern European countries (e.g. Russia, the Baltic States, Poland, Hungary and Slovakia) are taking as their models of future provision.

Basic characteristics

Welfare capitalism is a combination of:

- Keynesian values and economic instruments concerning the organisation, administration and regulation of the economy;

- a conception of welfare and welfare provision that uses universalistic principles and (predominantly) state-welfare programmes, and which seeks to ensure that 'all citizens have the resources needed to participate in the social (and economic) life of society'.

Welfare capitalism advocates:

- a mixed economy, that is, an economy with both a public sector (i.e. owned and/or regulated industries and services) and a substantial private sector;

- a government committed to Keynesian economics, committed, that is, to using the fiscal and monetary controls as a way of regulating the economy;

- state-financed and state-provided welfare;

- a free trade union movement that can pursue its objectives in a way that is compatible with the survival of a mixed economy and a Keynesian state.

The general economic goal of welfare capitalism is full employment. This, however, is not an end in itself; it operates in the service of a higher political goal that, for the moment, we can summarise as 'social justice'. Keynesian economic measures provide the state with the means of managing the economy. Managing the economy in a way that reduces instability, minimises unemployment and eliminates poverty, is seen as taking an important step along the road to social justice. The operations of the welfare state are regarded as treading a similar political path. They are designed to reduce the impact of unemployment where it exists, eliminate the extremes of poverty and generate a better quality of life.

They do so through:

- the provision of payments for the old, the sick, the disabled and the unemployed; and

- the supply of basic services – such as health, social services and education – to all of society's members regardless of their income, gender, class or ethnicity.

The support for welfare capitalism

Welfare capitalism's adherents range from reluctant supporters (academic conservatives like Beveridge and Keynes, and Conservative Party politicians such as Macmillan, Butler and Heath), through to positive advocates (academic Fabian socialists like T.H. Marshall, Titmuss, Townsend and Plant, and Labour Party politicians such as Atlee, Bevan, Crosland and Gaitskell).

The reluctant nature of conservative (and Conservative) support derives from the uneasy relation between state intervention in the economy (which both groups attempt to limit) and their concern to enhance the possibility of greater individual liberty. Basically, state intervention is seen to restrict individual liberty. But conservatives maintain better some compromise between individual freedom and state intervention than the vagaries of the free market. The spectre haunting conservatives (and Conservative adherents), is mass unemployment and the more specific instance of the degradation and poverty that beset Britain, Europe and America in the economic depression of the 1930s. Keynesian forms of economic intervention and the corresponding welfare state are seen to offer a safety net; inhibiting a repetition of such events (this indeed is what conservatives mean by 'social justice').

Socialist support for welfare capitalism operates from different grounds. It is a fundamental belief of Fabians that economic production and distribution should be subjected to governmental regulation in the pursuit of the higher political and moral goals of liberty and equality (the Fabian conception of 'social justice'). Economic regulation is an essential means of promoting social justice, or enhancing individual self-development and fostering a sense of community. The rationale for such regulation is provided through a contrast with free-market capitalism, welfare capitalism's recognised alternative:

> the free market is defective because the distribution of goods and services/income and wealth that occurs through the operation of the market does not secure social justice ... Given the inevitably random element in market outcomes, those whose needs are not met by the market have a defensible moral claim on the resources of those who are successful in the market. Hence, left to its own devices, the market causes injustice, an injustice which can only be rectified either by state intervention in the market ... or by the state providing an alternative to markets via welfare provision.

(Raymond Plant, in Le Grand, J. and Estrin, S. (1990), page 54)

In what follows, the major features of welfare capitalism are discussed through the arguments and proposals of its socialist advocates – the Fabians. After sketching the political values of the position, there will be a focus on its economics and its view of welfare policy and provision.

The political values of welfare capitalism

The central values

Because of the importance they attach to the role of ideas and ideals in history, Fabians have a lot to say about the kind of social values which they consider essential to socialism. They stress three central values – equality, freedom and fellowship – and two derivative values – democratic participation which is the child of equality and freedom, and humanitarianism which is the offspring of equality and fellowship ... these five [values] make up the basic value-mix of British democratic socialism.

(George and Wilding, 1985, pages 69–70)

By equality Fabians mean:

...more than a meritocratic society of equal opportunities ... more than a simple ... redistribution of income. We [want] a wider social equality embracing also the distribution of property, the educational system, social-class relationships, power and privilege in industry – indeed, all that [is] enshrined in the age-old dream of a more 'classless society'.

(Crosland, 1974, page 40)

Equality is an instrumental value; in other words, it is the consequences that are derived from implementing egalitarian policies that are important, not the notion *per se*. When such policies are successful, the outcomes are not simply greater equality but greater social integration, increased economic efficiency, better opportunities for self-realisation and greater freedom.

Greater freedom is valued in a non-instrumental way, if not the major value of welfare capitalism. We might best describe what Fabians mean by freedom through the use of Berlin's 'wall'.

Berlin describes two distinct kinds of freedom, positive freedom and negative freedom. By negative freedom, he means the absence of coercion:

Coercion implies the deliberate interference of other human beings within the area in which I could otherwise act. You lack political liberty or freedom only if you are prevented from attaining a goal by human beings. Mere incapacity to attain a goal is not lack of freedom.

(Berlin, 1969, page 122)

By positive freedom he means:

...the wish on the part of the individual to be his own master. I wish my life and decisions to depend on myself, not on external forces of whatever kind.

(Berlin, 1969, page 131)

Fabians have little time for 'negative freedom' mainly because it ignores what they regard as important barriers to liberty. Poverty, illiteracy and unemployment are examples of such barriers. They would be ignored by negative liberty because there is no implication of 'deliberate interference'. The Fabian philosopher Raymond Plant makes the point in this way:

> *The limitations on individual freedom are not just those imposed deliberately by intentional actions of others ... [there are] also those limitations which are imposed by natural differences of birth and genetic inheritance, together with those which are the result of human action, whether deliberate or not, in the field of family background, economic resources, welfare and education.*

(Plant, 1984, page 6)

For Fabians, the preferred conception of freedom is what Berlin terms 'positive freedom'. Positive freedom is a liberty that allows:

> *...me to live a meaningful life, to live it in my own way, shaped by my own values and purposes. This is a noble idea, and one which goes to the heart of what it is for a purposive creature to live a meaningful life.*

(Plant, 1984, page 6)

Fabians combine this notion of liberty with their instrumental conception of egalitarianism. Egalitarian policies should be designed to maximise individual freedom. Policies that counter poverty, racism, sexism, unemployment, illiteracy, and the social inequalities of having physical and mental disabilities ought to be designed to create 'equality of value' – equal dignity. By such means they should enhance individual liberty.

Closely linked with this conception of individual freedom (and therefore equality) is the Fabian notion of 'fellowship'. By fellowship they mean:

> *co-operation rather than competition ... the good of the community rather than the wants of the individual ... altruism rather than selfishness.*

(George and Wilding, 1985, page 74)

Democratic participation and humanitarianism complement the primary political values. Democratic participation enhances the Fabian belief in political and economic freedom. What it basically involves is the recognition that democracy should exist in all aspects of people's lives – in their work situations and in their local communities. Humanitarianism, in Fabian terms, involves the belief that there should be minimum standards of living and, further, that these minimum standards must be capable of alleviating the variety of forms of social stress to which people become subject. The clear corollary to this concerns the significance and level of welfare provision and the continued commitment to its maintenance.

These five values are often interwoven by Fabians through the general notions of citizenship and social justice. The state is the guarantor of equal liberty. It has to be concerned not only with political and civil liberties but also with the resources, opportunities, powers and rights which people need if they are to act as citizens. Welfare policies, it is maintained, should seek to be socially just; the just (egalitarian) distribution of social and economic resources enables those who are impoverished to exercise the freedom that the better placed have by virtue of income and education.

Free-market capitalism – The Conservative years 1979–1997

Free-market conceptions of society, the economy and politics dominated nineteenth-century political economy. In the twentieth century it:

> *lapsed into academic and political obscurity – particularly between 1940 and 1970. The (economic) recession which overtook many of the advanced industrial countries from the early 1970s however, encouraged a resurgence of [free-market] thinking. Its advocates – (such as Hayek) – gained a new eminence and influence.'*

(George and Wilding, 1985, page 19)

In the 1940s, 1950s and 1960s then, it was possible to regard free-market thinking as a system of thought belonging to another age. By the mid to late 1970s, however, such a viewpoint was no longer possible. Under Margaret Thatcher's leadership, initially in opposition and then in government, the Conservative Party revived and utilised free-market thinking as the basis of its economic, political and welfare policies. Quite why it developed with this change of leadership is a matter of speculation: after all, Enoch Powell was arguing a very similar kind of free-market thinking in the 1960s and it met with scant attention from those same politicians (Margaret Thatcher and Keith Joseph among them) who have openly embraced these views since the 1970s. Gamble offers the following explanation:

> *What made possible the rise [of free-market thinking] in the 1970s was the widespread perception in the [Conservative] Party that the Heath government had been a failure, and that Britain was becoming ungovernable. This coincided with the onset of world recession and increasing alarm about the implications of Britain's continuing relative decline. The climate of failure and indecision that clung to British governments in the 1960s and 1970s gave the political opportunity for a sharp break with both the rhetoric and practice of post-war [Keynesian] economics.*

(Gamble, cited in Levitas, 1986, page 49)

For Gamble then, it was less the intrinsic merits of free-market thinking than the perceived failure of Keynesianism that led the Conservatives under Margaret Thatcher's leadership to seek an alternative theoretical/philosophical terrain to that occupied by all governments since the Second World War.

A characterisation of the theoretical elements of Conservative free-market thinking

There are three elements to the free-market thinking propounded by Conservatives since the mid-70s. These are:

- libertarianism;
- The doctrine of economic individualism;
- The Austrian school's conception of liberal political economy.

Libertarianism

One of the best-known statements of this position is made by Robert Nozick. (See, for example, his Anarchy, State and Utopia.*) He argues that the minimal state, the state which protects the lives and property of its citizens, can be justified, but nothing beyond the minimal state. Any use of the state's coercive powers beyond this minimum infringes individual rights. Libertarianism carries hostility to government to its furthest extreme. Its concept of the economy is constructed on the basis of the absolute character of the property rights of the individual.*

(Gamble, ibid., page 30)

In many ways, libertarianism is the least significant of these elements. It occasionally provides both ministers and Conservative backbenchers with rhetoric – generally in their pronouncements of opposition to the quantity and cost of (central and local) government services – but it provides little more. Why? Because, as Gamble points out, the logical extension of the libertarian belief in the rights of individuals to own property, to create markets and to buy and sell whatever is wished without restriction, is also an effective justification for *free markets in heroin and pornography as well as (opposition to) controls on immigration*. This would be anathema to current conservatism and conflicts sharply with its commitment to an economic individualism (and its accompanying morality).

The doctrine of economic individualism

This is traditional laissez-faire (i.e. free-market) economics which assumes without question that markets are beneficial and governments harmful, and that individual freedom and government exist in inverse ratio to each other. The best-ordered economy is therefore one in which scope for individual choice is greatest and scope for government responsibility smallest. The level of taxation is the most important measure of this. The more taxed citizens are, the less free [they are].

(Gamble, ibid., page 30)

The doctrine of economic individualism with its commitment to market production and distribution, and its belief in economic choice is of some importance to current Conservatives and has led to the rejuvenation of ideas of self-help, competition and personal responsibility. Although it is of much greater significance than libertarianism, it is nonetheless of lesser importance than the third element – the Austrian school of economics.

The Austrian school of economics

The approach of the Austrian school of economics stems from the work of Carl Menger, but it is the specific work of one of Menger's students, Friedrich Hayek, which has been a major influence on British Conservatives' free-market thinking. The distinctive features of the school's approach are not simply its economics (in which it refused to accept the methodology of neo-classical positive economics or to focus attention on equilibrium theory) but its citing of economic issues within the wider context of political economy and, therein, its intractable opposition to socialist political economy.

> ### A caveat
> There needs to be care regarding language at this point. To speak of a source of ideas being 'a major influence' or 'having an impact' is not to suggest that the Conservative government's free-market thinking can be reduced to Hayekian first principles. Hayek's views did not determine or structure government policy in the previous Conservative government. They do not possess the status of edicts so much as guidelines for a free-market economy. They have been used by Margaret Thatcher and John Major in the development of economic, trade union and welfare legislation and policy.

Hayek's conception of political economy can be organised around the three central notions:

- freedom;

- the market economy;

- his opposition to welfare capitalism.

Freedom

Hayek makes it very clear that the political conception which is of paramount importance is the notion of freedom or liberty. In *The Constitution of Liberty*, Hayek defines freedom as the absence of coercion.

> *We are concerned in this book with that condition [of people] in which coercion of some by others is reduced as much as is possible in society. This state we shall describe throughout as a state of liberty or freedom. The task of a policy of freedom must therefore be to minimise coercion or its harmful effects, even if it cannot eliminate it completely.*

> (Hayek, 1960, pages 11–12)

> ### Note
> - The undivided nature of this conception of freedom, i.e. Hayek is not discussing particular freedoms or an aggregate of particular freedoms, he is saying that freedom is no more and no less than the absence of coercion.
> - Freedom's inverse relation with coercion: to maximise freedom we must minimise coercion.
> - That coercion concerns those situations in which people are forced to serve the interests of others, rather than pursue their own interests. It concerns the intentional actions of human agents.

Hayek believes that coercion by individuals is something that can be drastically reduced if one social agency, the state, is able to punish individuals who infringe laws governing individual exchange. But the problem then becomes one of how to reduce the coercion of the state itself. Hayek's answer is the construction of a private sphere free from public intervention. Such a sphere can only come into existence if there are certain activities and rights that are protected and cannot be infringed by government. This requires that:

- the government as well as individuals are bound by laws and that decisions of ministers, civil servants or other government agents can be subject to legal appeal and reversal in the courts;

- the government recognises the limits to its power through a conception of non-coercive government activity.

Such a conception, of course, conflicts with the idea of 'popular sovereignty' because it implies that there are laws that should be beyond the power of a government to alter. The doctrine of popular sovereignty would suggest that a government elected by the people has the right to overturn and redesign all laws.

Hayek's concern here is to preserve freedom by limiting the power of a legislative assembly, no matter how democratically constituted it is. He is not anti-democracy as such; indeed he sees it as the least harmful of governmental forms. For him, its benefits include:

- that it provides a peaceful way of resolving conflicts;

- that it provides the best way of educating people about public affairs;

- that it can act as a safeguard for individual liberty.

Nonetheless, democracy is flawed. In particular, it threatens freedom by creating the possibility of unlimited power for majority governments that could lead them into abuses involving increased state intervention.

The market economy

Defining freedom as he does, and expressing a degree of distrust in democracy as a result, leads Hayek to certain views of economic policy. In particular, he draws a simple equation between freedom and the market economy. The market is to be the sphere of free, voluntary, individual behaviour regulated by law and protected from the coercion practised either by individuals or the state. It is an economy in which the following conditions apply.

- Economic power is decentralised.

- The division of labour is co-ordinated by the market.

- Income is distributed through the free operation of market forces.

- The role of government is confined to the enforcement of those general rules, for example on contract and property that define the market order and make market relations possible. It needs to be vigilant and strong to enforce competition and outlaw private coercive power. But it has no role or justification in seeking to intervene directly in the decisions individuals take in the market.

Main suppositions

1 Hayek is committed to individualism; in other words, he does not accept that society possesses 'structures' (such as social classes) influencing the activities of people. Society is no more than an abstraction of the aggregate of individual activities. But what is it that maintains societal organisation? As you might guess from the preceding paragraphs, the answer is the role of law. Laws are necessary for both the operation of the market and the existence of individual liberty. They specify the grounds and conditions under which government would use its powers to protect individual economic and political liberty.

2 Market forces constitute the best mechanism for the production and allocation of goods and services in society.

3 Where there is need for some state provision of services, the extent of such public provision should be carefully specified and deliberately minimised.

4 Given that freedom is market freedom, the maximisation of market processes will also maximise political and economic freedom.

5 Markets work not on altruism but on individual self-interest. Competition is the 'keywork'; individuals compete in terms of both conflicting and common interests.

6 The individual pursuit of self-interest generates 'spontaneous co-operative activity', voluntary exchanges of goods and services. And since it is voluntary, exchange will only take place if both parties feel that they will benefit from it.

7 Free markets are more successful than planning in coping with uncertainty, because the knowledge available to planning authorities is nowhere near as great as the knowledge dispersed in a market among all its agents. Planning authorities would have no means of assessing whether their planning decisions were efficient or not, since prices would no longer be set by the forces of supply and demand (and thus by the competition between individual producers and consumers).

Hayek's opposition to welfare capitalism

Hayek's opposition to welfare capitalism is primarily based on an analysis in which his own views (of freedom and the market) are used as measures of Fabian proposals.

On planning and the economy

Planning in any form, whether in the older-style East European Communist planned economy or in the Keynesian conception of a managed economy, is regarded as an unnecessary and unwarranted intrusion that leads to a reduction of liberty. For Hayek, the institutional form of a market economy is not a political option; it is the mark of modern civilisation. Therefore it cannot be changed by political decree without threatening civilisation. This is why ideas of planning come in for such strong criticism. Planning is an atavistic move, a throwback to a more primitive way of life. It ignores all the complexities of the modern economic world that generated economic progress.

Of the managed economy

Capitalism, Hayek maintains, is about the creation of wealth by individuals taking risks in the market and launching new enterprises. Real aggregate demand in the economy, he argues, is an effect of production, not policy, Hence governments are powerless to affect real aggregate demand (in the way Keynesians suggest) through policies of taking and pending. What governments should be doing instead is encouraging entrepreneurial activities and the creation of wealth by reducing taxation.

All alternatives to markets are flawed

A great deal of effort has been devoted by the Austrian school (and Hayek in particular) to demonstrating that the basic ideas of socialism contain logical flaws, and further, that socialism cannot provide a rational means of economic organisation. Only an economic system based on private ownership can achieve an efficient allocation of resources and the greatest possible increase in wealth and productivity.

On equality

Hayek maintains that equality and freedom are usually at odds: to pursue equality is usually to suppress freedom. Equality generally demands state intervention and state intervention involves coercion. Given the paramount importance of freedom, general egalitarian policies must be abandoned.

In commenting on specific egalitarian policies (such as the redistribution of income through progressive taxation), Hayek suggests that they:

- discourage the creation of wealth;

- inhibit efficiency and productivity.

The only exceptions to his general stance on equality concerns are those equalities that are seen to enhance freedom, namely:

- civil and political liberties like equality before the law and electoral rights;

- equality of opportunity.

The rejection of social justice

Social justice, Hayek maintains, is not something that should feature in discussions of political economy. There is nothing just or unjust about market outcomes. What matters, for Hayek, is not the market's distribution of rewards but the conception of 'market order', based on general rules which guarantee everyone maximum opportunities. Actual distribution is a lottery – the chance of material inheritance and the manner in which opportunities arise. He defends this lottery approach to the market's distribution of rewards by maintaining that no better system can be devised. There are no principles of justice that permit a central authority to redistribute income more fairly. Redistribution undertaken by the state is as arbitrary as the system of rewards that it is trying to replace, and by legitimising intervention in the economy, it is being undertaken at the expense of freedom.

The attack on trade unions:

According to Hayek, trade unions have a legitimate role in society as voluntary associations, but their role should be strictly limited. In large-scale organisations, collective agreements on roles governing conditions of work, promotions and pay differentials may assist the smooth running of business. He also recognises the value of trade unions functioning as friendly societies insuring their members against sickness and unemployment. Unions become a problem and a threat to freedom, once allowed to develop beyond these functions:

> *Public policy concerning labour unions has, in little more than a century, moved from one extreme to the other. From a state in which little the unions could do was legal if they were not prohibited altogether, we have now reached a state where they have become uniquely privileged institutions to which the general rules of law do not apply. They have become the only important instance in which governments signally fail in their prime function – the prevention of coercion and violence.*

(Hayek, 1960, page 267)

Hayek makes the following claims.

- Unions have become private monopolies, able to pursue their objectives only by the coercion of some of their members or other workers.

- Unions *cannot in the long-run increase real wages for all wishing to work, above the level that would establish itself in a free market* (Hayek, 1960, page 270). Given this is so, he maintains that it therefore follows that if unions seek to raise wages above this level for some workers, they can only do so by harming others, by lowering their wages or forcing redundancies.

- The existence of national and industrial unions rather than company or plant unions, causes major damage to the economy; it distorts relative wages, restricts the mobility of labour and deters investment.

For the sake of freedom and the free functioning of the market order, trade unions must be returned to a status of small-scale (i.e. company – or plant-based) voluntary associations that cease from interfering with the manager's right to manage, or pursuing claims for increased wages above market valuations.

The welfare policies of free-market thinking on state welfare

State welfare is considered to supplant the free market:

- with its 'excessive' tax demands;

- by making itself a near-monopoly supplier in many welfare areas.

With its proliferation of services it is seen to undermine the family and individual responsibilities, and, with its system of benefits, to have produced a culture of dependency and irresponsibility.

What do free-market thinkers want in place of state welfare provision?

Ideally ... a situation in which the supply (of welfare services) is both competitive and privately owned, and (where) the demand (for services) consists of unsubsidised individual purchases.

(Hudson, 1989, page 1546)

Such an ideal is seen to have several advantages over current state welfare:

The advantage of the demand side is that people are able to maximise their individual welfare functions constrained only by their willingness and ability to pay, rather than by governmental budgetary constraint...

On the supply side the advantages arise from competition for customers and profits. This competition allows enterprises to satisfy consumer demand effficiently, by looking for profitable opportunities and seeking innovation.

(Flynn, 1989, page 105)

The political values underwriting this welfare mixture should be reasonably clear:

(M)arket mechanisms should be used wherever possible.

(Hudson, 1989, page 1546)

Sir Geoffrey Howe makes the point in the following way:

Putting markets and competition to work in the nation's interests is not just a policy for industry or local government. It is [also] an approach [for] the apparatus of the welfare state.

(From a speech in 1983, quoted in Loney, 1986)

- *(C)ompetition should be established between providers, even if this is largely the public sector competing within itself;*

- *(C)onsumers should be allowed to opt out of state provision in order to sharpen competition;*

- *(I)ndividualism and individual choice should take precedence over collective choices and planned provision;*

- *(I)f possible, individuals should manage without help from institutions of any sort, except their own families.*

(Hudson, 1989, page 1546)

(A)s a party committed to the family and opposed to the all-powerful state, we want people to keep more of what they earn, and to have more freedom of choice about what they do for themselves, their families and others less fortunate.

(Conservative Party Manifesto, 1987)

The Thatcher/Major-led governments used several instruments in pursuing these values that included:

- reducing public expenditure on statutory welfare services;

- privatising statutory services;

- shifting the expectations and the realities of care of:

  - the consumers of welfare services;

  - their carers/families;

  - welfare practitioners and their managers.

Welfare based on these values will, according to free-market thinkers, create a new agenda for welfare: an agenda that is both more realistic and which enables greater efficiency.

Social exclusion and paradoxes for social work

Social work universally appears to have its basis firmly rooted in a welfare capitalist ideology. There is almost universal acceptance that at its heart are notions of equality and freedom. Worldwide social workers attempt to counter discrimination of all kinds. Indeed the Central Council for Education and Training in Social Work (CCETSW) in England states in its Equal Opportunities Policy Statement:

> *Providers of social care and social work education and training and assessment centres will eliminate unfair discrimination and disadvantage in all aspects of their work regulated by the Council.*

(CCETSW, 1996)

However, as we have seen, a free-market capitalist system based on Hayek's principles is fundamentally opposed to society influencing the activities of people. It is committed to individualism where the individual is responsible for him/herself. If you pursue equality you will suppress freedom. Therefore given the paramount importance of freedom, general egalitarian policies must be abandoned.

Social work thus has no mandate for working towards creating equality, and the state should not be involved in this activity. Social work is thus reduced to a free-market commercial activity responding to individual consumer interests. Indeed, social exclusion will be seen as a positive indication that the market economy is working and is to be expected.

The only exception to this will be specific state-run or financed social work of the police-type social work within mental health or child protection.

The obvious conclusions for social work are thus at first sight quite depressing. However, perhaps one aspect has been forgotten by the free-market thinkers. It is the capacity for individual people to group together in communities/societies for the greater good of all. Perhaps individuals will look at their neighbours and decide to care for the entire human race; or will greed and the individual remain dominant?

The Third Way

The term 'Third Way' is not a new one and can be traced to Pope Pius the XII in the nineteenth century, who called for a third way between socialism and capitalism. Bill Clinton used the term in his 1998 State of the Union speech *we have moved past the sterile debate between those who say Government is the enemy and those who say Government is the answer. My fellow Americans, we have found a Third Way.*

Jordan (2000) suggests the term 'Third Way' has been adopted by Tony Blair's New Labour government as a name for its political philosophy and strategy. There has been a lot of debate over what is meant by the term the 'Third Way'. In a NEXUS-hosted online discussion in 1998, Stewart Wood (Fellow in Politics, Magdalen College, Oxford) stated that it represented *a form of political product differentiation without really knowing what the product is.*

One way of trying to understand the Third Way is by seeing it as a relationship between the individual and the community, and a redefinition of rights and obligations. It seeks to revive civic culture and utilise the dynamics of markets but with the public interest in mind.

Clearly there is some debate as to whether this is possible and, as previously mentioned, it could be argued that much of the welfare of the Third Way is directed towards the better-off as the marginalised in society do not tend to vote in general elections.

The politics of community and the third way

The concept of 'community' notoriously has many meanings: 57 according to Leaper in 1971. We can probably triple that number all these years later. Why the preoccupation to define community? Jordan (2000) argues that community has a key role in bringing together the two main moral traditions of individualist and collectivist ideology to create a Third Way morality for government at a macro level and service provision within health and social care at a micro level.

Individualism

Individualism is biased toward institutions that enable individuals to be responsible for themselves, to be morally autonomous, and to be committed to personal projects and relationships. It sees group ethics and collectivist institutions as intrusive and distorting of individuals' potential. It holds individuals to account for the outcomes of their decisions and choices. It sees justice primarily in terms of the procedures and rules that govern interactions, and therefore favours institutions such as markets and adversarial court hearings.

Collectivism

Collectivism is biased towards institutions that promote care, mutuality, solidarity and interdependence. It emphasises equality of membership, dignity and decency in all interactions, as factors enabling trust and co-operation. It sees individualistic ethics and morality as promoting selfishness and social irresponsibility. It holds individuals responsible for contributing to the common good, and restraining their competitive impulses. It sees justice in terms of the distribution process, as concerned with fair shares of the benefits of co-operation.

What the different meanings imply is that membership of a community involves a degree of reciprocity and co-operation, and mutual obligation and responsibility. In liberal political thought, a high priority is placed on individual freedom and on protection against interference or coercion by others or the state. Conversely, collectivism invests in the state with formidable coercive powers, involving strong restraint of individual liberties and interests, and an authoritarian role in the pursuit of common purposes, what Jordan (2000) describes as an 'objective' version of the 'good society' (page 50).

Therefore, community in a political and policy context is both a system of order and membership, and a way of getting things done; it is both a form of social organisation and a kind of economy. In the latter sense, as a way of producing and distributing goods and services, it is an alternative to markets and state services.

The Third Way focuses on community almost entirely as a system of social control, with members holding each other responsible for orderly conduct and work contributions, and thus providing the 'glue' to bind an inclusive society together (Williams, 1998).

New Labour, the Third Way and the welfare state

New Labour and the Third Way emphasise collaboration rather than competition and decreased reliance on market and quasi-market forces, long-term effectiveness rather than short-term efficiency.

Key principles for the reform of the welfare state are:

- an 'enabling' welfare state that promotes social and economic inclusion;
- the welfare state should address the causes of poverty and promote participation in the labour market;
- welfare policies should deliver social and economic inclusion and ease the transition from welfare benefits to paid employment;
- a skilled workforce is crucial to a national competitive efficiency;
- rather than a redistribution of wealth and income, the role of the state is to provide citizens with opportunities for education and training thus enhancing individual life chances.

Commentators have argued that New Labour's focus on paid employment does not deal with inequality. The idea of labour market inclusion uncritically accommodates the wealthy in the 'in work' majority and thus fails to challenge existing distributions of wealth and power. It presents an overly homogenous image of society in which many inequalities exist. The emphasis on paid employment does not recognise unpaid work, such as caring or parenting, as a legitimate contribution to society.

New Labour argue that the New Right's attempt to withdraw the state and promote individualism and markets eroded communal and co-operative values. In contrast, New Labour's welfare programme embodies the idea of citizens, linked together by reciprocal duties and responsibilities, who collaborate with the state in a co-operative enterprise to ensure an economically vibrant country.

They call for greater accountability founded on co-operation and partnership focusing on managerial techniques that build on partnership and strategic alliances. They also call for decentralisation, flexibility, freedom from bureaucracy, entrepreneurialism and local autonomy.

Welfare revolution: True or false?

In the 60 years since the inception of the welfare state, all aspects of social services have been targets of unprecedented masses of legislation, much of it creating new powers, duties and responsibilities for social services. During the last decades of the twentieth century, a second revolution in social policy could be said to have taken place, as many welfare services were reconstituted and privatised and markets were created for the purchase and delivery of services. Local government was subjected to transformation by complex arrangements involving the public, private and voluntary sectors.

Have any of these changes significantly improved the quality of life for specific groups of individuals? On the whole, those who already have wealth and are higher earners have fared well. However, according to Powell and Hewitt (2002), welfare policies during the twentieth century have left the living conditions of many of the worse off largely unchanged.

Powell and Hewitt go on to suggest there is evidence that unemployment, inadequate housing, deficient health and community care, low incomes and problems associated with poverty still particularly affect people experiencing physical or learning disabilities, older people, people with mental health problems, lone parents, those with less earning capacity, children in poor families and families living in resource-starved urban and rural districts where access to welfare services are far from adequate.

The poor are still viewed with a mixture of sympathy and suspicion, depending on the extent to which they are regarded as trying to help themselves. Stereotypes of the homeless beggar, the 'morally' deficient single parent (usually a mother), the 'dangerous' 'mad' person (who fluctuates between mad, bad or sad), the disabled person deemed as a lesser person as they do not meet the 'norm' physically and/or mentally, or the older person 'past it' and invisible to society are still dominated by prejudices rather than informed realities of their circumstances and the experiences of people themselves.

The focus on the undeniable changes in the welfare services, and how they are organised, managed and delivered, diverts attention from the unchanging realities of being poor, being alone, experiencing health problems, becoming older and living in a society which discriminates against people who are different, whether through class, gender, age, ethnicity, disability, sexuality or any other social division.

From New Labour to a coalition government

There are a number of key texts which evaluate the impact of New Labour's reform to the welfare state since 1997, when the Labour party came to power. (See Jordan, 1998, 2000; Powell and Hewitts, 2002 Clarke et al., 2000).

One of the interesting aspects of social policy development has been the emphasis on 'welfare to work'. Here the welfare state has been used to encourage people back to work, so that they cease to be a burden on society. One could argue that the reduction that has been seen in unemployment figures is a testimony to the effectiveness of this strategy.

However, as is considered in Chapter 7, this has a consequence in the number of people available to work in informal care and thus it increases the pressure on community care.

Another aspect of the welfare policy under New Labour was the emphasis on targets and tables, in an attempt to increase the quality of care in certain areas. For example, there is much attention to the needs of the acute ill-health sector and casualty waiting lists, with a host of strategies mentioned elsewhere in this text as to how best 'improve' this situation. But there is little emphasis on the marginalised groups and 'Cinderella' areas such as learning disabilities. Indeed one could draw the conclusion that the aim of New Labour welfare policy is to move away from free-market principles towards a welfare capitalist system for those services that meets the needs of the middle-class voters while providing few new resources to those marginalised within society other than an encouragement to seek employment to reduce the burden on society.

This movement of the value base for the welfare system produces a fundamental dilemma for social work practice if social work sees itself as a profession with a core value to work to promote equality and to attempt to eliminate inequality. The value base of social work thus comes into conflict with the value base of the welfare policy of society.

At the time of editing of this second edition, the UK has ended up with a coalition government. During the election process we experienced for the first time a live televised debate between the three main political leaders.

New words and phrases have come into common usage since the banking and financial sector turmoil of 2008. We now talk about 'credit crunch' and 'global recession' in ways which were hardly considered a few years ago. In the public sector, services have come to the end of this three-year comprehensive spending review (CSR) of October 2007 and this public spending to date has not really been affected by the 'credit crunch'. However, financial spending in the public sector will be significantly affected by the Autumn 2010 CSR, which will have impact from April 2011.

Clearly there is a huge pressure to reduce public spending and this will have a significant effect on health and social care expenditure. Yet this will occur at a time of even greater pressure for resources fuelled by demographic ageing, the rise in the number of people with conditions such as Alzheimer's disease and a society which is constantly expecting high-quality services and more from the state. So we are likely to see even more privatisation of services (which is really rationing by any other means) and an even greater move towards 'personalisation' of services to prevent people coming into 'residential care' (DoH, 2008). Of note here: although politically we are told that the preventative service will save money by keeping more people in the community, over time the service users will of course get older and often their condition deteriorates to the extent that they will eventually require residential care for complex needs. Thus we may see a financial saving in the short term, but in the medium term there will be significant cost on pressures to care for those citizens.

In summary, social work will feel even greater pressures to find resources and to advocate on behalf of vulnerable adults and children. Yet there remains a big and important challenge for the profession and this text is written to support you, the social work professional, to better understand the important task of working with people in our society.

The various chapters in this book look at and consider this issue and hopefully they will help you as a social worker to consider your own value base while also helping to equip you with a clear basis on which to base your social work practice upon.

As a final point, we saw in the lead up to the 2005 general election the ultimate irony of a Conservative opposition leader, Iain Duncan Smith, suggesting that, if elected, a Conservative government would abolish university tuition fees while the Labour government proposed to raise the fees (Webster and Owen, 13 May 2003).

REFLECTION POINT

- Which political party has its roots in the free market and which party has its roots in the welfare state in the twenty-first century? This confusion is often a major issue when looking at welfare policy and social work delivery in Britain.
- Which of these parties reflect social work perspectives?
- To end, we ask amid the complexities of social work practice in the twenty-first century, how do you perceive yourself as a professional and how does this impact on your practice, and what has influenced you most as a professional in practice and why?

Chapter 2

The changing face of community care: Assessment, personalisation and outcomes

Dr Lee-Ann Fenge

Introduction

Community care has become a popular concept over the past 30 years and there is a substantial amount of law and policy which structures this area of practice. The White Paper Caring for People defined it in the following way:

> Community Care means providing services and support which people who are affected by the problems of ageing, mental illness, mental handicap or physical or sensory disability need to be able to live as independently as possible in their own homes, or in 'homely' settings in the community.

> (DoH, 1989, page 3)

What is 'community care'?

Twenty years have elapsed since this definition appeared and an array of new legislation and policy has been developed to guide community care decision- making. In recent years this has reflected a shift towards a pedagogy of personalisation (Hartley, 2008) and the increasing involvement of service users and carers in the control of their care. This presents a vision of social care in which individuals are helped to maintain their independence by giving them greater control and choice over the ways their needs are met (DoH, 2005b, 2006a). This approach to personalisation is resulting in service users and carers being required to use their skills and capacities to develop and manage their own packages of care through individual budgets, direct payments and person-centred planning (Manthorpe et al., 2008).

However, despite this shift in emphasis, it is claimed that community care *appears to be in substantial disarray* (Mandelstam, 2009, page 39). Mandelstam (2009, pages 40–2) identifies eight factors which contribute to this current disarray. These are:

- lack of adequate resources;

- a mismatch between need and available resources resulting in help being withdrawn;

- a gap between official policy and practice which results from a failure to concede the extent of inadequate resources;

- performance targets resulting in a distortion of priorities;

- a complex and uneven legislative framework;

- the use of legal escape routes used by local authorities and NHS bodies to reduce their perceived obligations;

- a growing focus on protecting and safeguarding adults;

- professional good practice being undermined by the pressures and uncertainties inherent in the community care system.

An example of this disarray is evident in the Mental Capacity Act 2005, Deprivation of Liberty Safeguards and people with dementia. The Deprivation of Liberty Safeguards came into force in April 2009 aimed at protecting the liberty of people lacking capacity who are admitted to institutional settings in England and Wales. This should promote the development of institutional care which encourages autonomy in order to prevent deprivation of liberty. However, it is suggested that insufficient resources and a reduction in regulation and inspection have prompted a system where economic efficiency is prioritised over safeguarding the right to liberty (Boyle, 2009).

This highlights how resources continue to dictate the types of responses that those in receipt of care receive. This chapter will explore some of the current tensions in the field of community care policy and practice, and the implications this has for practitioners.

Care management and the transformation agenda

The role of the 'care manager' has been a central feature of community care for nearly two decades. Care management and assessment were identified by the 1989 White Paper *Caring for People*, as being 'the cornerstone' of high-quality care (Cmnd. 849, para.1.11). Practitioners increasingly find themselves dealing with the inevitable tensions that arise in terms of undertaking assessments within constraining and changing organisational contexts. Personalised social care through increased choice provides further complexities and contradictions for frontline practitioners.

The transformation agenda is transforming the social relationships that currently exist within the field of social care. This signifies a major shift in the provision of social care, and the government's drive towards personalisation can be seen as an approach which empowers individuals to shape their own lives and the services they receive. This has implications for practitioners, users of services, and those who may care or advocate on their behalf. The personalisation of social care provision through self-assessment and individual budgets is challenging existing power relationships, resulting in the potential for users of services to have far more control over care (DoH, 2005b). This shift is clearly explained in the recent Social Care Institute for Excellence (SCIE) report of 2008 which suggests that *personalisation reinforces the idea the individual is best placed to know what they need and how those needs can be best met* (Carr, 2008, page 3).

Direct payments were introduced by the Community Care (Direct Payments) Act 1996 and came into being in April 1997 for adults of working age. They were extended to older people in 2000. The introduction of direct payments in 1997 was focused on providing users of social care services more direct control and economic choice over their care needs (Spander, 2004). The payment must be sufficient to enable the service user to purchase services to meet their needs, and must be spent on services that users need. Scourfield (2007) suggests that direct payments can be viewed in the context of a 'bottom-up' struggle organised around the goals of empowerment, independence, choice and control. However, he warns that there is more to service user 'self-actualisation' than simply going it alone through control of an individual budget, and the nuances between independence and dependence need to be acknowledged.

Individual budgets were first mooted in January 2005 in a paper by the Prime Minister's Strategy Unit, as a way of personalising services. However, at the time a similar idea was already being piloted by the *In Control* programme, which was set up in 2003 by Mencap and the Department of Health's Valuing People Support Team and initially targeted at people with learning difficulties. *Putting People First* (DoH, 2008) is the culmination of a policy process that began with the adult social care Green Paper, *Independence, Wellbeing and Choice* (2005b), and was developed through the health and social care White Paper *Our Health, Our Care, Our Say* (2006a). This initiative set out the role of adult social care services and the role they have in increasing people's independence and inclusion in local communities. Self-assessment is a key feature of this approach and is increasingly seen as the starting point for helping people to express their expectations of service provision (their outcomes) in terms of the benefits that it will bring them.

'Outcome'-focused assessment in contrast to 'needs-based' assessment is therefore a key feature of undertaking assessments which seek to involve service users in identifying the outcomes they wish to achieve (Nicholas, 2003). Assessment does not occur in a vacuum, and as policy changes, the nature of assessment itself is altered. For community care practitioners, the transformation agenda focuses greater emphasis on the roles of brokerage and advocacy rather than assessor discretion within the assessment and planning process (Foster et al., 2006). This in turn may have implications for the sustainability of personalised social care which is reliant on an understanding of the complex assessment processes which operate at the service user/practitioner interface.

Care managers are faced with a tension between their professional values of 'user empowerment' and shared ownership of the assessment process with service users, and the restrictions imposed by agency accountability and funding criteria (Fenge, 2001). This may have implications on the assessment process leading to tensions between the outcomes that the service users want and what can be achieved in terms of the service context. Research undertaken by Foster et al. (2006) suggests that *practitioners' awareness of the constraints and limitations of the resource context influenced the assessment process and their decision making* (Foster et al., 2006, page 131).

ACTIVITY 1

Think of your own practice context. What informs the way in which you approach assessment?

What differences might there be between 'outcome'-focused assessments or 'self-assessments'?

Assessment

Assessment is an essential role within community care practice since the NHS and Community Care Act 1990 placed a statutory duty on social services to assess the needs of those who may require community care services. The knowledge base of social work practice, alongside the policy and practice context of community care, has a major influence on the ways in which practitioners undertake assessment. Social work has been criticised for uncritically importing knowledge from other disciplines, and it has been suggested that *borrowed knowledge from psychiatry and psychology has been the major influence on social work practice* (Milner and O'Byrne, 1998, page 25). It has also been suggested that assessment within care management is further restricted by an emphasis on bureaucratic procedures which emphasises more procedural models of practice and the 'administrative' process (Lymbery, 2005). The disabled people's movement has also been critical of the ways in which policy and practice have traditionally focused on an individual approach to disability in which disabled people are defined by their medical and individual needs rather than rights as citizens (Swain et al., 2004; Oliver and Sapey, 2006).

The transformation agenda is now promoting a process of self-assessment in which the assessment is undertaken by the service user themselves with their own desired outcomes of care. This shift is clearly explained in the recent Social Care Institute for Excellence (SCIE) report of 2008 which suggests that *personalisation reinforces the idea the individual is best placed to know what they need and how those needs can be best met* (Carr, 2008, page 3). While younger disabled individuals are embracing this change (Glendinning et al., 2008), older people remain reluctant to engage with it. Therefore differences based on the age of the service user may influence the experience of self-assessment and individual budgets.

Historically, social work departments in the UK have structured their work with older people on the basis of ageist assumptions; oversimplifying their needs as being routine (Hugman, 1994). Older people have been defined by professionals in terms of their dependency or frailty (Clark and Spafford, 2002), and the language of dependency and risk has been used to structure assessments, which disempowers older people further (Richards, 2000). A recent evaluation of the Individual Budgets Pilot Programme (Glendinning et al., 2008) suggests that many older people do not want the additional burden of planning and managing their own support, and that *it may take time for older people to develop the confidence to assume greater control* (Glendinning et al., 2008, page 19). This position is reinforced by research into the poor take-up of direct payments by older people (Commission for Social Care Inspection, 2004). These findings suggest that many older people may be reluctant to take control of their own care, and perceive this shift to self-assessment and control of individual budgets as risky and something to avoid. In a more positive vein, other research has suggested that individual budgets can have positive outcomes for older people in rural communities, including paying for transport to access activities and paying local people to work for them (Manthorpe, 2008).

Despite a shift towards personalisation and self-assessment, it is likely that vulnerable people will still be entitled to have their personal budgets and packages of care managed for them by local councils (Pitt, 2009), adding a further layer of complexity to the role of care managers.

ACTIVITY 2

In what ways is a move towards personalisation and self-assessment changing your practice?

What might be some of the challenges to supporting service users with self-assessment?

What does this mean for the way in which you work alongside service users and carers?

Assessment of need/outcomes

A system of self-assessment and personalised budgets suggests that service users will have more control over their care outcomes. However, a system which is simply designed to offer more choice is meaningless unless individuals are furnished with sufficient information in order to be able to make informed decisions (Corrigan, 2005). There is a need for agencies to provide information in appropriate formats, and that this information should be targeted and easy to find. Research suggests that users of information prefer it to be tailored to their own specific circumstances (Baxter et al., 2008). There is an onus of responsibility for agencies to provide clear and accessible information to those who are being offered choice and control over their care so that they can make informed decisions about their needs and the options open to them.

The concept of need is central to community care and both policy and practice guidance refers to 'needs-led' assessment. Local authorities are left with the power to decide what services might be provided to meet need. Section 47(1) of the NHS and Community Care Act states:

> *Where it appears to a local authority that any person for whom they may provide or arrange for the provision of community care services may be in need of any such services, the authority – (a) shall carry out an assessment of his/her needs for those services; and (b) having regard to the results of that assessment, shall decide whether his/her needs call for the provision by them of any such services.*

The concept of 'need' itself is problematic, and has been used to denote 'individual need' as well as the wider 'needs of society'. This encompasses notions of individual versus collective need. Do we have a common understanding about what a need actually is? Any discussion of need has to explore the social and political context in which the definition is constructed.

How we assess need may depend to a large extent on how we approach the concept. Liss (1998) describes two different approaches to the assessment of need.

- *Tension need* – need is viewed as tension or a disequilibrium – needs are satisfied when tension is eliminated. If we assess need using the 'tension' approach we assess what people actually strive for.

- *Teleological need* – need in this context is related to a certain goal, and the need is a lack of something or a gap related to a certain goal. To assess using this approach is to assess what things are necessary to achieve a certain goal.

These different approaches will impact upon the solutions offered to service users in terms of responding to the definitions service users might use, versus professional definitions of what resource is required to meet a need.

One model which has proved useful when exploring different definitions of need within community care practice is Bradshaw's taxonomy of social need (1972). In this chapter it will be applied to consideration of a move towards personalisation and self-assessment.

Bradshaw's taxonomy of social need

Bradshaw (1972) suggests that the concept of 'social need' is inherent in the idea of social service. He describes how four classes of need can be used in the process of policy formation:

1 normative need;

2 felt need;

3 expressed need;

4 comparative need.

Normative need
Bradshaw defines normative need as that which:

> The expert or professional, administrator or social scientist defines as need in any given situation.

> (Bradshaw, 1972, page 640)

A desirable standard is laid down and this is then compared with the standard that actually exists. The normative definition of need is subject to the value judgements of the 'expert'. In many situations 'expressed' or 'felt' need is not considered a valid indicator of need until it has been legitimised by an expert. The traditional system of assessment within community care can be seen as a system in which 'experts' were actively involved in the assessment and prescription of services on behalf of service users. Personalisation and self-assessment introduce a more subjective element to this process of assessment. Needs and outcomes are defined by the service user themselves and there is a potential that long-term quality of life is improved by service users being offered more choice and control, moving the focus of the assessment away from routine personal care to encompass broader aspects of well-being (Netten et al., 2007). This policy emphasis and philosophical basis of personalisation facilitates a reduction in the demarcation between professionals and non-professionals (Leadbeater and Miller, 2004), and a view of service users through the self-assessment process as experts by experience.

Felt need

In this situation, need is equated with want. Bradshaw suggests that:

> *Felt need is, by itself, an adequate measure of 'real need'. It is limited by the perception of the individual.*

(Bradshaw, 1972, page 641)

Felt need is therefore focused on people's subjective perceptions of need. It will be influenced by the format of assessment and the questions used to structure it ('would you like'/'do you want'/'do you need'). It will also be influenced by comparisons people make with their peers and other groups. The perception of the individual is an important element in the self-assessment process. Through a process of 'co-production' between the service user and practitioner it is recognised *that people who use services have assets which can help improve those services, rather than needs which must be met* (Needham, 2009, page 1). The challenge for practitioners is to support services users in their self-assessments so that 'felt need' can be expressed in terms of desired outcomes.

Expressed need

According to Bradshaw (1972), people have an expressed need if they feel a need for a service and have requested or demanded that their need be met. He suggests that:

> *Expressed need or demand is felt need turned into action.*

(Bradshaw, 1972, page 641)

Examples would be waiting lists in the health service or housing departments. Expressed need may also be voiced by groups, voluntary organisations, political parties, etc., and pressure groups can be influential in identifying new needs. However, it is also important to remember that often the people most in need may have the greatest difficulty in expressing their needs. A focus on 'desired outcome' rather than just on a need for a service as suggested by Bradshaw may enable a more creative approach towards personalisation. However, as mentioned earlier in the chapter, it is important that individuals are furnished with sufficient information in order to make informed decisions or assessments of their care requirements (Corrigan, 2005; Baxter et al., 2008).

Comparative need

A measure of comparative need is obtained by studying the characteristics of the population in receipt of a service, if some people are in receipt of a service and others in similar circumstances are not, then the latter are considered to be in need. When the four classes of the taxonomy are applied to individuals, need may be indentified as being present or absent by each definition in turn. As a result individuals will be found to fall into 1 of 12 categories of need. However, tensions may be perceived in such a model where definitions of need are framed differently by policy makers or professionals, and those that feel or express their needs. In the current economic climate, where there is an emphasis on fiscal restraint and spending reviews, it is likely that such differences will become more extreme, and eligibility for services more restricted.

Risks and rights

In recent years 'risk' has become a central concern for both policy and practice. Although the rhetoric of community care supports the idea of a needs-led assessment, Postle (2002) suggests that the context of care management has been influenced by three main factors: restricted resources, operating within a market for care, and risk. Therefore alongside assessment of need, risk and the assessment of risk are key concerns for staff in social care organisations. The assessment of risk covers the difficult areas of 'protection', 'rights' and 'responsibilities'. Milner and O'Byrne (1998) suggest that the differing emphasis on risks, needs and resources has made it difficult for social work to develop an overarching framework for all their assessments.

Recent policy and guidance have put the focus on risk centre-stage within social care practice. This includes *Risk, Responsibility and Regulation: Whose Risk is it Anyway?* (Better Regulation Commission, 2006), *Making Choices: Taking Risks* (Commission for Social Care Inspection, 2006) and *Independence, Choice and Risk: A Guide to Best Practice in Supported Decision Making* (DoH, 2007). However, despite the term 'risk' being used within the arena of social care, it is difficult to find clear definitions or criteria about what is actually meant by this term. Risk is often perceived in negative terms, and the policy response has been to provide safeguards and avoidance of potential harm to vulnerable groups (Titterton, 2005). However, a move towards more personalised care necessarily means that the benefits of risk-taking need to be explored (Alaszewski and Horlick-Jones, 2004).

A policy shift towards personalisation of care and individual budgets leads to a transfer of power for managing risk from services and organisations to service users and their families (Mitchell and Glendinning, 2008). The promotion of choice and control for service users over their care outcomes assumes that service users want choice and the opportunity to take risks. However, there are tensions within this process as professionals still retain statutory duties and are required to strike a balance between promoting the rights of the individual and a 'duty of care' (Kemshall, 2002).

The issues around choice and risk are complex. Not only is the picture complicated by different understandings or definitions of risk, but eligibility criteria and resource availability may also complicate this area of practice. A focus on risk to independence is stressed within the Fair Access to Care Services (FACS) guidance. In England, local authorities are required to follow central government guidance on 'fair access to care' and to *assess peoples needs in terms of risks to their independence* (Mandelstam, 2009, page 151). Risks to independence are categorised as critical, substantial, moderate or low. However, the setting of thresholds means that not all needs or risks will be met (Mandelstam, 2009).

ACTIVITY 3

What guidance is used within your practice context to inform the assessment of risk?

In what ways may a move towards self-assessment and personalised care create tensions in the domains of risks, rights and needs?

The DoH guidance *Independence, Choice and Risk* (2007) offers a 'common approach' for social care practitioners in achieving a balance between rights and responsibilities, and the subjective experiences of service users. This guidance provides the following useful definition, which reiterates the important of working closely with service users in any decisions concerning risk:

> *A decision about the perceived or actual risk needs to be taken in conjunction with the person using services themselves, as well as the professionals involved. Just as taking a risk is a personal choice, levels of risk are perceptions, and a judgement about an acceptable level of risk should be a joint decision.*

(DoH, 2007, page 11)

The governing principle behind good approaches to independence, choice and risk is that people have the right to live their lives to the full as long as that does not prevent others from doing the same. To put this principle into practice, people supporting users of services have to:

- help people to have choice and control over their lives;

- recognise that making a choice can involve some risk;

- respect people's rights and those of their family carers;

- help people understand their responsibilities and the implications of their choices, including any risks;

- Acknowledge that there will always be some risk, and that trying to remove it altogether can outweigh the quality of life benefits for the person;

- Continue existing arrangements for safeguarding people.

(DoH, 2007, pages 12–13)

Vulnerability

The notion of vulnerability is important. It suggests the need for protection. If an older person is considered to be vulnerable, taking risks may be actively discouraged because it is felt that the individual needs to be protected from danger.

For certain client groups, the impact of discrimination may increase the view of 'vulnerability' and decrease the likelihood of risk-taking. Conrad (1992, cited Phillips, 1996) suggests that welfare institutions have tended to treat all their older clients as dependent and thus in a negative light, and this can lead to *justification for ever-increased intervention* (page 135).

Recent legislation has offered increased protection to vulnerable adults in terms of their rights to be supported to make their own decisions. The Mental Capacity Act 2005 provides a statutory framework to empower and protect vulnerable people who are not able to make their own decisions. It makes clear who can make decisions, in which situations, and how they should go about this. Guidance on the Act is provided in a Code of Practice. The Act came into force in 2007. See Chapter 3.

Five key principles underpin the Act.

- A presumption of capacity – every adult has the right to make his or her own decisions and must be assumed to have capacity to do so unless it is proved otherwise.

- The right for individuals to be supported to make their own decisions – people must be given all appropriate help before anyone concludes that they cannot make their own decisions.

- Individuals must retain the right to make what might seem as eccentric or unwise decisions.

- Best interests – anything done for or on behalf of people without capacity must be in their best interests.

- Least restrictive intervention – anything done for or on behalf of people without capacity should be the least restrictive of their basic rights and freedoms.

The law already presumes capacity and the Act reasserts this principle, but also provides that anyone involved in someone's care/treatment can assess and conclude that the subject is incapacitated on the basis of 'reasonable belief'. The Act replaces existing statutory schemes for enduring powers of attorney and Court of Protection with reformed and updated schemes.

The Act deals with the assessment of a person's capacity and acts by carers of those that lack capacity.

- Assessing lack of capacity – the Act sets out a single clear test for assessing whether a person lacks capacity to take a particular decision at a particular time – a 'decision-specific test'. No one can be labelled 'incapable' as a result of a particular medical condition or diagnosis.

- Best interests – the Act provides a checklist of factors a decision-maker must work through in deciding what is in a person's best interests.

Although the Mental Capacity Act 2005 presumes capacity until proven otherwise, it is likely that ambiguities and challenges will remain for practitioners, particularly around the issue of 'best interests' (Mitchell and Glendinning, 2008).

The future

The role of the 'care manager' has been central to the community care assessment process for the past 20 years. However, a move towards a pedagogy of personalisation and self-assessment offers a challenge to the traditional role of the care manager. Within the growing policy context of personalisation, there is an emphasis of co-production alongside service users' values, the individual's subjective experience of the assessment process and the outcomes they desire as a result of it. This offers a challenge to practitioners, and new skills may be needed to support the service user in the 'authorship' of their self-assessment. Gorman (2000, page 15) warns against a focus on the technical aspects of work to the exclusion of the emotional and suggests that *such an approach denies care managers the opportunity to meet individual needs in a holistic way and to make empowering practice a reality*. Part of this challenge may include the ability to support service users to think creatively about their care needs and the ways in which these can be met.

Social care modernisation through the processes of personalisation and self-assessment *open up ambiguous political spaces* (Newman et al., 2008, page 553). Progressive agendas growing out of service-user and advocacy groups have become incorporated into policy through initiatives such as personalisation, self-assessment and individualised budgets. However, Newman et al. (2008, page 553) warn that these agendas might be vulnerable to co-option within neoliberal approaches to privatisation and individuation. This may lead to ongoing dilemmas for practitioners as they navigate between the need to promote choice and independence, while practising within a service environment which is risk-averse or financially constrained. It is likely that the move towards personalisation and individual budgets will add to the complexities of community care practice for practitioners and service users alike.

Chapter 3

The Mental Capacity Act 2005

Michael Lyne

Introduction

This chapter will offer practitioners a general overview of the Mental Capacity Act 2005 (MCA). For a more detailed understanding of the provisions, any of the texts by Ashton et al. (2006), Bartlett (2005) or Jones (2005) in the reference list are recommended. The Code of Practice is essential reading for professionals and others working with those who may lack capacity to make certain decisions. Practitioners are also guided towards the website of the Office of the Public Guardian which contains a wealth of useful information regarding the Act, including downloadable and printable booklets and leaflets which can be given to service users.

The chapter starts by placing the Act in its historical context and then investigates the prevalence of incapacity. It outlines the principles of the Act before exploring the main ways in which decision-making can be achieved either by those with capacity to make relevant decisions or on behalf of those that lack such capacity and professionals' roles within these processes. Finally there is a brief description of the criticisms which have been levelled against it and its role in the 'safeguarding' process.

The origins of the Act

The Mental Capacity Act 2005 was a long time in development and its enactment has been widely welcomed by most commentators. It is agreed by most that reform of the law in this area was overdue. Drivers for reform have included the legal context, demography, improvements in healthcare, developments in policy, particularly in community care and the field of the protection of human rights.

In some respects, one has to part the curtains of time and look back to the reign of Edward II in 1339 to place this Act in context. *Parens patriae* jurisdiction or the Royal Prerogative, given statutory recognition in that year (the earliest acknowledgement seems to date from 1324), gave the High Court jurisdiction over the rights of adults lacking capacity.

The *Report of the Royal Commission on the Law Relating to Mental Illness and Mental Deficiency 1954–1957,* cited in Bartlett (2005), investigated the area of statutes relating to this, and its recommendations were partly implemented by the 1959 Mental Health Act, which removed the Royal Prerogative in respect of adults, which could only be used on an individual basis. Instead it established a statutory jurisdiction, providing a legal process which could be applied for those who needed it without the intervention of either the monarch or the courts. However, a side-effect of the 1959 Act was to deprive the courts of jurisdiction over welfare and healthcare decisions other than for mental disorder.

A number of other pieces of legislation, both concurrent with the 1959 Act and pre-dating it, including the Lunacy Act 1890 which established what became known under the 1959 Act as the Court of Protection, left the area of capacity in a state of *incoherence, inconsistency and historical accident* (Law Commission, in Jones, 2005) The Law Commission's investigation into the state of the law revealed that it offered insufficient protection for the rights of people who lacked capacity to manage their affairs or for those carers who might be managing affairs on behalf of another, as there was no single piece of legislation or process which could be applied uniformly and easily understood by all concerned.

The practical result of this was a lack of clarity in regards to decision-making on behalf of people who lacked capacity, especially in relation to matters dealing with health and welfare. A raft of cases went before the courts, including *Re F (Mental Patient: Sterilization)* and *Airedale NHS Trust v Bland,* which dealt with persistent vegetative states. However, for less serious issues, much reliance was placed on the use of the common law. Decisions made under common law were made with the clear understanding that the incapacitated person's best interests should be the overriding guide in the decision-making process. However, what was less clear was the demarcation between continually acting in a person's best interests against committing an assault if the act was repeated.

At the same time it was acknowledged that England and Wales have an ageing population and that there is a correlation between ageing and loss of capacity. This is not to say that every older person loses capacity to make decisions, but that the prevalence of such a loss rises with increasing age.

Couple this to advances in medical science, such as antibiotics and increases in survival rates for diseases such as cancer, which now save the lives of people who would previously have died, and the potential numbers of incapacitated people can be seen to be rising. This is reflected in paragraph 2.38 of the Law Commission paper which noted that the:

> *Achievements of medical science have also created difficult dilemmas about the appropriate measure of medical care which should be given at the end of life, particularly where unconscious or incapacitated people have, in advance, indicated an unwillingness to be kept alive once their health has deteriorated.*

> (Jones, 2005)

Policy developments have led to changes in the way that people are cared for. The National Health Service and Community Care Act 1990 has directed service providers to avoid institutional care for the most part, decreasing the paternalistic mode of care in favour of increasing individual responsibility for decision-making. However, if we assume that numbers of incapacitated people are likely to rise, and indeed, recent research from the Alzheimer's

Research Trust has indicated that there may be as many as 820,000 people currently suffering from dementia in the UK (Luengo-Fernandez, Leal and Gray, 2010), then this policy direction is likely to mean that provisions of the MCA are called on more frequently.

The importance of achieving clarity in this area of legal and clinical practice cannot be overstated. As capacity issues potentially affect every member of the population, it is in everyone's interests that the Act is fit for purpose and user-friendly. No one can know whether they will retain the mental acuity to make even the simplest decisions in later life. Equally, no one can be sure that they will not suffer an accident or illness that removes their decision-making faculties at any time. Provisions within the Act should be welcomed by all, while at the same time acknowledging the concerns of some commentators that the Act is not as robust as it could have been (Jones, 2005).

The Mental Capacity Bill's passage onto the statute books was not without difficulty. Perhaps the major stumbling block was the insistence on advance decisions to refuse treatment being legally enforceable. An advance decision allows a person, who has capacity, to decide in advance which treatments or forms of treatments they would not want should they subsequently lose capacity and be unable to act for themselves. This can include refusal of life-sustaining treatment if certain criteria are followed when drawing up the document.

However, this was taken by many in Parliament to be a move allowing euthanasia.

> *Richard Kramer, co-chair of the* Making Decisions Alliance *... said there was a real danger that the benefits of the bill could be overshadowed by high profile debates around euthanasia. Concerns focus on advance statements, which allow people to refuse treatment, according to the General Medical Council's definition including artificial nutrition and hydration.*

> (Anon, Community Care Magazine 2004)

The most vociferous opponents to this section of the Bill were the Bishops sitting in the House of Lords who could not, in all conscience, vote for a Bill which allowed the ending of life, however positive its other effects might prove to be. The Prime Minister at the time, Tony Blair:

> *personally intervened yesterday to save the government's mental capacity bill, striking a last minute deal with the Catholic church by promising that the bill will not allow euthanasia by the back door. Mr Blair held telephone conversations with the Archbishop of Westminster, Cardinal Cormac Murphy-O'Connor, while Lord Falconer, the Lord Chancellor, held parallel talks with Peter Smith, the Catholic Archbishop of Cardiff.*

> (Wintour, 2004)

It is perhaps indicative of the importance of the Bill to the government that they did not allow the Bill to die at this stage but came to a reasoned settlement of the difficulties.

> *Tony Blair was eventually required to provide assurances that the Act would not alter the law relating to murder, manslaughter, and assisted suicide, and at the last moment section 62 was added to that effect.*

> (Barlett, 2005)

Section 62 outlines the scope of the Act and contains many of the words in the quotation above but also specifically relates the MCA to the Suicide Act 1961, specifying that nothing in the MCA alters that Act (Bartlett, 2005).

The Act defines a person's lack of capacity thus: *a person lacks capacity in relation to a matter if at the material time he is unable to make a decision for himself in relation to the matter because of an impairment of, or a disturbance in the functioning of, the mind or brain. It does not matter whether the impairment or disturbance is permanent or temporary.* (MCA 2005 section 2 subsections 1 and 2).

In light of this definition, it can be seen that the numbers of people in England and Wales to whom the Act might be useful at any given moment is vast. The Act uses a two-stage test to assist in deciding whether someone lacks capacity but by accepting that a lack of capacity can be a temporary condition, it also encompasses those people in difficulty because of an acute infection, for instance, as well as the more recognised serious difficulties posed by dementia and other longer-term conditions. It should be noted though that most of the main provisions of the Act only apply to people aged 16 and over. Indeed, some provisions only apply to over-18s.

The prevalence of incapacity

Research into the prevalence of incapacity and the reliability of incapacity assessments has tended to concentrate on two separate groups: firstly, medical (or surgical) inpatients and secondly, psychiatric inpatients. The question asked in most of the available studies is 'does the patient have the capacity to make a treatment-related decision?'

In 2004, Raymont et al. investigated the prevalence of incapacity among a group of medical inpatients. In a sample group of 302 patients the researchers discovered that approximately 40 per cent did not have capacity.

Perhaps more worryingly, the researchers identified that clinical teams rarely spotted this lack of capacity or tested for it. *Our study suggests that in routine clinical practice, doctors most usually fail to identify that patients with significant cognitive impairment do not have capacity* (Raymont et al., 2004).

Cairns et al. (2005) studied the prevalence of incapacity using psychiatric inpatients. Although the researchers in this study used a smaller group of participants than the Raymont study, they still discovered that approximately 43 per cent lacked capacity. They discovered that patients detained under the Mental Health Act 1983 (MHA) were significantly more likely to be lacking in capacity and that the majority of patients judged to be lacking capacity had either a psychosis or bipolar disorder.

The five principles

The principles of the Act are encompassed on the face of the Act itself within section 1, which is designed to set the ethos of the law, which is to protect people who lack capacity to make their own decisions and to ensure that individuals are encouraged to participate in the decision-making process whatever their state of mind or health.

The presumption of capacity, the first principle, was well enshrined in common law and this has become more accepted in latter years but one doesn't have to look back too far to see that this wasn't always so. The phrase 'Mrs Jones doesn't have capacity because she is suffering from dementia' is still sometimes heard. This should be challenged as although someone with dementia may not be able to make life changing decisions they may still be able to make everyday ones.

The phrase is also challengeable on the basis that capacity is time- and decision-specific so should be phrased as 'Mrs Smith does not have capacity to make this decision at this time'. The burden of proving that a person lacks capacity falls upon the decision-maker at the time.

The Act further encourages practitioners in the second principle, to take all practicable steps to help an individual make their own decisions. Things to take into account here may include the use of translators for people whose first language isn't English or for people with hearing problems who might need sign language. Different techniques might be needed when working with someone with a learning disability. A speech and language therapist may be needed if the person has physical difficulties regarding talking. Attention should also be paid to the environment in which the decision-making is happening.

The third principle governs the individual's right to make an unwise decision without having their capacity brought into question. The difficulty for practitioners will be in deciding when an unwise decision becomes a potentially dangerous one to the point where intervention may be necessary in the person's best interest following an assessment of capacity. It should not be forgotten that individual decisions which appear eccentric or unwise should not call that person's capacity into question but if looked at cumulatively, a pattern of such decisions may indicate an issue with capacity.

The fourth principle, acting in a person's best interest, is not a new one and indeed is a further example of the common law being placed on a statutory footing within this legislation. This principle is perhaps the most fundamental one in the Act.

The fifth principle deals with the concept of achieving a similar result in terms of outcomes but by using a less restrictive alternative. There is an expectation that in having regard to this principle, practitioners should consider whether there is any need to intervene in the first place.

Decision-making by and on behalf of vulnerable adults

Section 5

Section 5 of the Act clarifies the common-law 'doctrine of necessity' and provides protection against liability for practitioners who carry out acts in connection with care and treatment assuming that the person lacks capacity and the act has been carried out in the person's 'best interests'.

'Best interests' is not a new concept. In years gone by, professionals may have decided on what was in someone's best interests based on their knowledge of the person, their knowledge of the person's illness or condition or on their own professional knowledge and skills.

The Act now gives practitioners a process to follow so that they can gather evidence and arrive at a decision which has taken all the circumstances into consideration and one which can truly be said to be reflective of the person's own wishes where possible and certainly in their best interests. The process is explained in Chapter 5 of the Code of Practice in what is known as the 'best interest checklist'. The Code of Practice in electronic form is available at **www.publicguardian.gov.uk**.

By following the best interest checklist and ensuring that recording of capacity assessments and decision-making processes is detailed, practitioners can defend themselves against 'wilful neglect or ill treatment', which is a criminal offence under section 44 of the Act.

Section 5 might be used, for instance, to provide personal care or giving an essential injection to a person who does not have capacity to agree to the intervention.

Lasting Powers of Attorney

Lasting Powers of Attorney (LPA) allow a person to give decision-making powers to another person in the event that they lose capacity. There are two types of LPA; Property and Affairs and Personal Welfare. LPA in relation to Property and Affairs are a replacement for the old Enduring Powers of Attorney (EPA) which can still be legally binding. However, no one can make a new Enduring Power of Attorney. LPA in relation to Personal Welfare allows the attorney to consent to treatment on the person's behalf.

LPAs must be made while the person has capacity to make the decision. The relevant forms can be downloaded from the Office of the Public Guardian website and completed following the guidance notes. While there is no requirement to obtain legal advice, it may be prudent to engage the services of a solicitor if the person's life or requirements are particularly complex.

The attorney is a person of the individual's choice. There can be more than one attorney. They can be asked to act individually or in tandem or individually for some decisions but not others. It is also a good idea to name a replacement attorney in case anything happens to the first. The LPA can be as detailed or as general as the maker themselves wishes.

The document has to be 'certified' by a third party and before the LPA becomes legally binding it has to be registered at the Office of the Public Guardian. There is a fee for this. See the website for the current rates. There is also a statutory period between the receipt of the document by the Public Guardian and its registration which allows for any objections to be made by persons who have been listed on the document as people to be notified.

Practitioners must see the actual document before accepting decisions from people who claim they hold power of attorney. This is to ensure that the document is registered and to clarify exactly what powers the attorney has and under what circumstances.

The Court of Protection

An arm of the High Court, the Court of Protection has the power to decide whether a person has capacity to make a particular decision for themselves; make declarations, decisions or orders on financial or welfare matters affecting people who lack capacity to make such decisions; appoint deputies to make decisions for people lacking capacity to make those decisions; decide whether an LPA or EPA is valid; remove deputies or attorneys who fail to carry out their duties, and hear cases concerning objections to register an LPA or EPA and make decisions about whether or not an LPA or EPA is valid.

The Court is the final arbiter for complex cases. Should it prove impossible to come to a conclusion about a decision or should there be a dispute about a decision, then the Court can be approached for a resolution. However, applications to the Court can be expensive and despite the stated intent of the Court being informal and quick, it has been shown that some decisions are taking time to be handed down. The Court needs to be seen as a last resort and should really only be considered where the decision to be made might have serious consequences to the person's life. Recent decisions from the Court have included decisions about the registration of LPAs and some decisions regarding deprivation of liberty.

If someone loses capacity and hasn't made an LPA, then the Court can appoint someone to make decisions on the person's behalf. This person is known as a 'Court Appointed Deputy' and will often be a family member, for instance a son or daughter who is given access to the person's bank accounts and can therefore pay bills, etc. However, deputies have to act with the best-interests principles in mind and can be removed by the Court should it be proved that they are acting inappropriately.

The Public Guardian and the Office of the Public Guardian

The role of the Public Guardian is to protect people who lack capacity from abuse. The Public Guardian, supported by the Office of the Public Guardian (OPG), helps protect people who lack capacity by, among other things, maintaining a register of Lasting Powers of Attorney (LPA) and Enduring Powers of Attorney (EPA); maintaining a register of Court Appointed Deputies; supervising Deputies; asking Court of Protection Visitors to visit people who may lack capacity and those who have formal powers to act on their behalf such as Deputies; receiving reports from attorneys acting under LPAs and from Deputies; and providing reports to the Court of Protection and dealing with cases where there are concerns raised about the way in which attorneys or Deputies are carrying out their duties.

Advance Decisions to Refuse Treatment

It has long been a point of law that adults with capacity have the right to refuse treatment or parts of treatment. Advance Decisions to Refuse Treatment places this right on a statutory footing.

Advance Decisions must be made while the person has capacity and can only be made by people over 18. They can be verbal or written down. If they are about life-sustaining treatment they must be written down and signed, they must be witnessed and they must have a statement included on the document saying something like *This advance decision stands even if my life is at risk*.

Advance Decisions must be 'valid' and 'applicable'. Validity means that the person must not have acted in any way which is inconsistent with the decision since making it and must not have withdrawn it. Creation of an LPA giving the attorney the authority to consent or refuse to treatment in question after the creation of the Advance Decision will also make it invalid. Applicability means that:

> *There are reasonable grounds for believing that circumstances exist which the maker of the advance decision did not anticipate at the time of its making and which would have affected his or her decision had he or she anticipated them.*

(Ashton, et al., 2006)

The Advance Decision may also be inapplicable if the person has the capacity to consent to or refuse the treatment in question at the time the treatment is needed, if the treatment falls outside that specified in the decision or if any circumstances specified in the decision are absent.

The known existence of an Advance Decision does not stop practitioners offering treatment to patients even if they know of such a decision. As well as having the right to refuse treatment, capacitated adults have the right to change their minds and accept treatment even though they may have previously indicated they wouldn't. It is good practice to check the patient's wishes on each occasion that treatment is indicated.

Advance Decisions can be made in order to refuse psychiatric treatment. Persons admitted voluntarily to hospital for treatment for mental disorder have the legal right to have their Advance Decision respected. However, the situation changes if the person is detained under the Mental Health Act 1983. In these circumstances any Advance Decision in relation to mental disorder should be taken into account when making treatment decisions but can be overruled by the mental health team if appropriate. The only exception to this is if the Advance Decision relates to electroconvulsive therapy (ECT) which can only be overruled if it is for the purpose of using ECT to save the person's life.

Useful further reading in this area is the *Reference Guide to Consent for Examination or Treatment* (DoH, 2009a).

Research

The Act contains provisions in relation to carrying out research with the involvement of people who lack capacity. Chapter 11 of the Code of Practice describes the steps which must be taken in order to fully comply with the Act but can be summarised as follows:

Research covered by the Act cannot include people who lack capacity to consent to the research unless:

- *it has the approval of 'the appropriate body', and*
- *it follows other requirements in the Act to:*
  - *consider the views of carers and other relevant people*
  - *treat the person's interests as more important than those of science and society, and*
  - *respect any objections a person who lacks capacity makes during research.*

(Code of Practice 11.9)

In addition, research needs to be linked to the impairing condition that affects the person who lacks capacity, or the treatment of that condition, and there have to be reasonable grounds for believing that the research would be less effective if only people with capacity are involved, and researchers have made arrangements to consult carers and to follow the other requirements of the Act.

Independent Mental Capacity Advocates

Independent Mental Capacity Advocates (IMCAs) safeguard the rights of people who:

- are facing a decision about a long-term move or about serious medical treatment;

- lack capacity to make the specified decision at the time it needs to be made;

- have nobody else who is willing and able to represent them or be consulted in the process of working out their best interests, other than paid staff. The Act calls people in these circumstances 'unbefriended'.

Regulations under the Mental Capacity Act give local authorities and NHS bodies powers to involve IMCAs in other decisions concerning:

- a care review;

- adult protection procedures (even in situations where there may be family or friends to consult).

IMCAs are independent and generally work for advocacy providers who are not part of a local authority or the NHS. Staff working in local authorities or the NHS must be able to identify when a person has a right to an IMCA and know how to instruct an IMCA.

The first step is to know which organisation has been commissioned to provide an IMCA service in the area where the person currently is. This information can be found out from the local authority or from information and advice centres such as the Patient Advice and Liaison Service (PALS) or the Citizens' Advice Bureau (CAB).

The IMCA will:

- establish the referred person's preferred method of communication;

- meet with the referred person and use a variety of methods, as appropriate, to ascertain their views;

- consult with staff, professionals and anyone else who knows the person well who are involved in delivering care, support and treatment;

- gather any relevant written documents and other information;

- attend meetings to represent the person, raising issues and questions as appropriate;

- present information to the decision-maker verbally and via a written report;

- remain involved until a decision has been made and be aware that the proposed action has been taken;

- audit the best-interests decision-making process;

- challenge the decision if necessary.

Criminal offences under the MCA 2005

Section 44 introduces the offences of wilful neglect or ill-treatment, the potential punishment for which is up to five years in prison. As well as imprisonment, a fine can be imposed.

This section applies to all persons who are looking after someone who lacks capacity. This includes professionals, unpaid carers, family, friends, etc. The best defence against this charge is that the accused was acting in the person's best interests. For this reason it is important that careful and detailed recording of the best-interests process should be undertaken by professionals.

Statistics from the Crown Prosecution Service show that in 2008–2009, 43 cases were prosecuted and reached at least a first hearing in a magistrates court (CPS, 2009). At least two people have received custodial sentences as a result of being found guilty of a section 44 offence in a crown court (The Law Pages, 2010).

The Deprivation of Liberty Safeguards

The Deprivation of Liberty Safeguards (DoLS) were introduced into the MCA 2005 by the Mental Health Act 2007 as a result of the 'Bournewood' case (HL v UK [2005] 40 EHRR 32). The case concerned a man who lacked capacity who was admitted voluntarily to a mental health unit and then kept there.

'Deprivation of liberty' is only half a sentence. In order to put it into its proper context one should always add on the second part of the phrase, which is 'deprivation of liberty contra to Article 5, European Convention on Human Rights' (ECHR).

Article 5(1) gives a right to liberty and security and says that liberty can only be taken away as long as it is done using a procedure set out in a nation's laws. The person being deprived of his or her liberty also has to fit into a group, also outlined in Article 5. These groups include criminals and, for this purpose, 'persons of unsound mind'. The usual 'procedure prescribed by law' for persons of unsound mind in England and Wales is the Mental Health Act 1983.

Article 5(4), ECHR, gives a right to a legal review of any deprivation of liberty. Criminals, under certain circumstances can appeal against conviction and sentence. Persons detained under the MHA can appeal to either a panel of hospital managers or the First Tier Tribunal (Health, Education and Social Care Chamber), previously known as the Mental Review Tribunal.

In the Bournewood case it was successfully argued that HL had been admitted to a hospital without the use of a procedure prescribed by law and further, he had no recourse to appeal that admission.

The procedure for depriving a person of their liberty under the Safeguards contains a six-part assessment and a review process. Deprivation of liberty will be time-limited. The six parts are age, mental health, mental capacity, best interests, eligibility and no refusals assessments.

The process is relatively straightforward to follow on paper. If a hospital or care home, the 'managing authority', considers a person who lacks capacity is being, or is in danger of being, deprived of their liberty, they have to ask the 'supervisory body' for authorisation to deprive the person of their liberty. If the person is in a care home then the supervisory body will be the relevant local authority. If in a hospital it will be the primary care trust (PCT).

Upon receiving a request for authorisation, the supervisory body must commission the six-part assessment. The assessment has to be carried out by a minimum of two people with an Independent Mental Capacity Advocate appointed for the 'unbefriended'.

The first part of the assessment is ensuring that the person is aged 18 or over. The Safeguards do not apply to children or young people.

Secondly, the person has to be assessed to see whether they are suffering from a mental disorder within the meaning of the Mental Health Act 1983. This part of the assessment has to be carried out by a registered medical practitioner who is either approved under s12(2) MHA 1983 or who has special experience in the diagnosis and treatment of mental disorder. *The mental health assessor is required to consider how the mental health of the person being assessed is likely to be affected by being deprived of their liberty, and to report their conclusions to the best interests' assessor* (Ministry of Justice, 2008).

The mental capacity assessment can be undertaken by anyone who is eligible to act as mental health or best-interests assessor. The question being asked in this part of the assessment is whether or not the person lacks capacity in relation to an agreement to be in the hospital or home for the proposed or ongoing care or treatment.

The best-interests part of the assessment will be undertaken by certain health and social care professionals who have undergone specific training regarding deprivation of liberty. In some respects the best-interests assessor plays the most pivotal part of the assessment. The purpose of this part of the assessment is:

> *to establish whether deprivation of liberty is occurring, or is going to occur, and, if so, whether it is in the best interests of the relevant person to be deprived of liberty, whether it is necessary for them to be deprived of liberty in order to prevent harm to themselves, and whether such detention is a proportionate response to the likelihood of the relevant person suffering harm and the seriousness of that harm.*

(Ministry of Justice, 2008)

The question of whether the person is being or is going to be deprived of their liberty is patently the most crucial question in the whole process. If the best-interests assessor decides that no deprivation of liberty is occurring or is going to occur, then there is no need for the assessment process to proceed any further. The assessor will have access to care plans and any relevant assessments and will also have to seek the views of family members, carers and any professionals involved in the case. They will also have to consider the findings of the mental health/mental capacity assessor.

The eligibility assessment is linked to the mental health assessment. It is likely that any inpatient who lacks capacity to agree to be in a hospital or care home, who has a mental disorder within the meaning of the Mental Health Act 1983, would and possibly should be detained under that Act. Anybody who is detained in hospital under that Act would be ineligible for an authorisation under the Safeguards.

The final part of the assessment is the 'no refusals' assessment, the purpose of which is *to establish whether an authorisation to deprive a person who lacks capacity to consent would conflict with other existing authority for decision making for that person* (Ministry of Justice, 2008) such as an Advance Decision to Refuse Treatment which relates to some or all of the treatment proposed or if the authorisation would conflict with any decision made by an attorney or court-appointed deputy.

Assuming that all parts of the assessment support an authorisation for deprivation of liberty, the best-interests assessor must decide how long the authorisation should last for, the maximum length of time being for up to one year.

The best-interests assessor should also recommend someone to be appointed as the person's 'representative':

> *The role of the relevant person's representative, once appointed, is to maintain contact with the relevant person and to represent and support the relevant person in all matters relating to the operation of the derivation of liberty safeguards ... if appropriate triggering a review ... or making an application to the Court of Protection.*

> (Ministry of Justice, 2008)

So as to provide the patient with speedy access to a court for a review of the lawfulness of their detention as per Article 5(4), the patient or someone acting on their behalf has the right, within certain parameters, to make an application to the Court of Protection for a ruling on aspects of the authorisation or the assessment process.

If at the end of the authorisation period the person is still in need of being deprived of their liberty then the managing authority will need to request a further authorisation.

Should a request for an authorisation be turned down during or following the assessment process, the managing authority will need to take steps to ensure that they do not deprive the patient of their liberty illegally. It should be noted that use of DoLS does not necessarily equate to poor care. For some people, relevant, appropriate and good care may still amount to a deprivation of their liberty.

Recently released figures from the NHS Information Centre indicate that by December 2009, 1,074 people had been made subject to an authorisation under the Safeguards.

Criticisms of the Act and its role in the safe-guarding process

Some of the major criticisms of the Act relate to what some commentators see as 'gaping holes' in the protection of vulnerable adults. The Act emphasises the need for individuals to make their own decisions wherever possible and sets out procedures for acting on the behalf of those who are not able to decide for themselves. However, some people have commented that there is not enough protection within the body of the legislation.

In fact, the OPG (Office of the Public Guardian) is required to supervise people making decisions using an LPA or EPA and those people can be removed by the Court of Protection. There are safeguards in terms of research with people who lack capacity. There is a criminal offence punishable by imprisonment. Certain people have a right to independent advocacy.

For those who are deprived of their liberty, there are the Deprivation of Liberty Safeguards which, if nothing else, should encourage managing authorities to pay more attention to the care-planning process and person-centred care as key to the prevention of depriving people of their liberty is to ensure that they retain as much autonomy as possible. One criticism is that DoLS does not apply in people's own private homes. Any deprivation of liberty discovered in these circumstances would need to be dealt with either via the safe-guarding process or the police.

The Act itself dovetails nicely with the safeguarding process and can be used to enhance it. Protections exist within the Act. It is up to society to decide whether it wants to use them fully.

Conclusion

This chapter has provided an overview of the main provisions of the MCA 2005 and Deprivation of Liberty Safeguards. It has highlighted a number of areas where practitioners may have obligations and responsibilities. Practitioners should also be aware of and investigate their own employer's policy and guidance in relation to the Act. Many employers have provided paperwork which can be usefully used in order to assess capacity and make best-interest decisions. As with other areas of health and social care, careful, detailed and good-quality recording of actions taken under the Act will lead to a successful outcome for the person who lacks capacity.

Chapter 4

The older person's social care and the enabling service

Professor Keith Brown

Introduction

The National Health Service (NHS) and Community Care Act of 1990 and the gradual policy adjustments which prepared for it after 1988 (Robinson and Le Grand, 1994) had clear implications for the care of disabled and dependent elderly people in terms of funding, decision-making, responsibility for care, and professional roles. The outcomes experienced by elderly people and their families are less clear and this chapter will attempt to explore some of the implications of social policy for the recipients of services.

The care of elderly people is located in the contested ground between the values of free-market individualism and the politico-economic imperative of central control of public spending (George and Wilding, 1994; Hills, 1997) between social and healthcare (Twigg, 1997; Redfern, 1998), and between the conflicting power claims of professional management and the medical and allied professions (Harrison and Pollitt, 1994). The needs of the elderly may therefore provide a sharpened focus for analysis of the interplay of ideologies and interests within care provision and its implications for recipients.

It is not intended to take an historical perspective, but to select particular aspects of the ideology behind the reforms of the late 1980s and early 1990s which seem to bear especially on the relationship between elderly people and the organisation and control of health and social care.

The politico-ideological background

The main doctrinal assumptions, discussed by George and Wilding (1994) on which the neoliberal-capitalist welfare reforms of the Thatcher government were based may be summarised as follows.

- The welfare state is economically damaging because it increases public spending and therefore the tax burden of the productive individual and of competitive business. In doing so it reduces enterprise, incentive and economic growth and so reduces the wealth of all levels of society, including the very poor.

The emphasis on productive elements in society targets, for reduction of expenditure, groups who are unavoidably unproductive including the elderly and disabled. An increase in national wealth, it is argued, will improve the well-being of all and so issues of citizenship and social justice are subservient to growth in the economy (Dean, 1996).

• The welfare state creates a dependency culture and thereby impedes the entrepreneurial independence of outlook on which GB plc depends for its competitive edge.

The 'dependency culture' concept in relation to the elderly implies that families have come to see care of elderly relatives as the duty of the state and should now be asked to take back a responsibility they have avoided. In fact families, principally women, have cared for the majority of elderly people (Hills, 1997) but the changing nature of the family, especially through increased divorce and serial marriage and the expectation that women work, is increasing the need for state support.

• The welfare state is intrinsically expansionary and resistant to politico-economic control.

With regard to healthcare, the expansion of medical technology and tradition of professional autonomy have been seen as a major inflationary factor, as well as a culture of increased expectation and demand for medical intervention as an individual social right. The resultant government policy has included managerialisation of the NHS in order to challenge professional power on behalf of government and to introduce a framework of measurement as a basis for rational, transparent decision-making.

Clarke and Newman (1998) argue that this has resulted in a new power struggle between managers and government and reduced democratic accountability. Vulnerable groups, defined as 'wicked issues', are problematic in this scenario because their needs are complex and rarely measurable in output terms and they tend to cross organisational boundaries. They cannot be defined in terms of core business and so have low priority in the ethos of rational management (Clarke and Newman, 1998; Harrison and Pollitt, 1994; Clarke, 1998).

• Political planning of the economy is both impossible and damaging to the natural and efficient operations of the market. The free market knows best and without it, as in the centrally controlled welfare system, inefficiency and waste are inevitable.

Applied to the NHS where there is no direct purchaser-consumer, this principle has resulted in a quasi-market that has been seen as creating more administrative waste and discontinuity of services, though its benefits have been an increased transparency of cost issues and emphasis on quality improvement (Robinson and Le Grand, 1994).

• State paternalism towards the individual, however altruistic and whether administered through professionals or bureaucracy, is always an untenable intrusion into the right to freedom from interference, the only admissible freedom. The consumer knows best and must be freed to make choices in the welfare market.

The resultant mix of tight political control of resources and economic freedom of market forces which is linked with individuated rights and consumer-led services, has been seen as the origin of tensions and contradictions in the welfare policy reforms of the Thatcher government (Morgan, 1998; Clarke and Newman, 1998). The creation of self-governing, but budget-limited, NHS trusts contains the conflicting elements of lack of democratic accountability through dispersal of power and yet tighter financial control from the centre.

Rationing

The attempt to identify a consumer who has real choices in order for an internal market in health and social care to be self-regulating has resulted in the acceptance of a quasi-market compromise with socially and organisationally divisive consequences which may reduce the cost-efficiency and consumer orientation which were its main overt aims (Morgan, 1998; Clarke and Newman, 1998). The creation of new demand for services inherent both in competition for patients in the primary care sector and in the systema-tisation of care management and need assessment, is concurrent with reduction of the means to meet demand and increased public awareness of rationing.

All these issues are problematic in rendering operative what is a fundamental dichotomy (Clarke and Newman, 1998; Bartlett et al., 1994; Morgan, 1998).

It is self-evident that state financial resources are finite. Rationing is inherent to the safety-net concept of the welfare state (Morgan, 1998; Dean, 1996; Clarke and Newman, 1998). That the limit of those resources is likely soon to be exceeded by an uncontrollable welfare demand has been effectively countered. Hills (1997), from a survey of research findings and international comparisons, shows that the British welfare state is relatively economical and able to sustain such *upward pressures on welfare spending* as might be expected in the next 50 years. In particular, the NHS compares well in cost-effectiveness with most of Europe and the United States. Morgan (1998) asks in similar vein, *is 7.1% of GDP really an adequate amount to be spending on our health care?*

However, Hills does link his optimistic view of future resources to economic growth and it is not certain how spreading recession as a result of market collapse in East Asia might impact on Western economies (Ricupero, 1998; Shipman, 1998). Neither does he deny that the future of welfare provision is problematic given the conflicting political impera-tives already mentioned.

That welfare spending is out of control and a danger to the health of the economy might be construed as a political truth and as such informs policy as part of a new political consensus, called by Clarke and Newman (1998) *the Thatcher settlement*. The liberal-capi-talist doctrine that public spending increases individual and corporate taxation and so saps enterprise and economic growth (George and Wilding, 1994), the foundation of the wel-fare reforms of the Conservative governments (Butler, 1994), appears, in modified form, to underpin the fiscal and welfare policies of New Labour. There remains a commitment to at least hold taxation constant, and initiatives such as the proposed NHS trust mergers for example, are justified on the grounds of cost-cutting (Morgan, 1998).

The elderly as 'bed-blockers'

The emphasis has changed. The concerns remain the same and are the all-pervasive back-ground to organisational and professional decision-making in health and social care and especially to the support of long-term dependent groups such as the elderly. Despite Hills' debunking of the myth of the 'demographic time bomb' (1997), the perceived problem of the increasing burden of elderly people, surviving to frail old age in greater numbers, continues to define the elderly in a negative, pejorative way.

Elderly people have been disadvantaged by the intensification and strategic development of rationing within the welfare reforms in several ways. The purchaser/provider split which deepened the divide between healthcare and social services through the mechanism of conflicting budgetary needs, redefined the dependent elderly person as the 'bed-blocker'. The need for NHS trusts to show optimum use of beds and the managerial concentration on outputs rather than outcomes has focused healthcare attention on earliest possible discharge and questioned the rationale for longer than average hospitalisation (Clarke and Newman, 1998; Jones, 1998). Clarke and Newman (1998) describing the role of the NHS trust manager as focusing on the requirement to manage demand, and see the broader management debates around bed-blocking as a direct result of the emphasis on the measurable which derives from the output definition of efficiency.

Social service departments, by contrast, intent on operationalising the policy of a needs – rather than provision-led service, have a requirement for a slower process to allow for tailor-made care packages to be created for each user (Lewis and Glennerster, 1996). It is in this area of policy-created culture conflict that the tension between the directives both to create an enabling-consumer empowering service, to cut costs and to increase measurable efficiency, that has implications for vulnerable groups and for interprofessional working, can most clearly be seen.

The role of care manager in assessing individual need, and planning and organising support, is both enabling and gatekeeping. It is also operating in a process designed to maximise consumer input into decision-making, and control has clearly been devolved to that recipient/professional interface. Mayo (1994) describes the difference of perspective between health and social services concerning at what point assessment should be carried out. For care managers it is important that the assessment is valid and remains so, as far as is possible, over time. Waiting for the consumer to reach a state of some stability is a necessity, both to ensure that the right decision is made and to limit costs.

For the hospital, the imperative is to discharge from the bed at the earliest possible moment because, as Clarke and Newman point out, output not outcome is the measure of managerial efficiency, and a longer than average stay is a measurable cost that is not linked directly to an output. The managerialisation of the NHS is explained, by both Clarke and Newman (1998) and Harrison and Pollitt (1994), as an attempt to control health spending by reducing the ability of professionals to demand limitless funding for their prescribed treatments. In the hinterland between social and healthcare there is scope for vulnerable people to be reclassified in order that they become the responsibility of a different budget-holder.

In a needs-led social service, based on the complexity of care management operating in a dual role as gatekeeper and social worker, and directed to prioritise care in the home, and a managerialised and output-orientated health service, interprofessional collaboration between the services becomes problematic. The climate of rationing and competition intensifies a fundamental conflict of interests (Mayo, 1994; Jones, 1998; Twigg, 1997).

Transfer to the private sector

The tightening of the criteria for hospital care to prioritise acute medical care and give a low priority to higher dependency, slower turnover, less medicalised healthcare need has effectively placed care of the elderly largely outside the universal element of the welfare state (Redfern, 1998; Jones, 1998). Twigg (1997), discussing the phenomenon of the social, i.e. not medical care, points out that healthcare is free at the point of delivery while social care is means-tested and contributory, or indeed, seen as a private concern. There is a political as well as a managerial organisational agenda.

Jack (1998) discusses care in the community in relation to the anti-institution consensus that defines institutions as buildings, and as always and exclusively depersonalising and debilitating, i.e. institutionalising in their outcomes. He identifies a diminishment of choice consequent to the closure of local authority residential provision and the capping of local government spending, which led to predominantly private or voluntary-sector provision of residential care with no obstacle to *merger and marginalisation of the small provider*. Jones (1998) also claims that local authority funding of the private sector has led to closure of small homes and favoured monopolistic consortia. Mayo (1994) and Jack (1998) challenge the definition of community that excludes residence in a building other than the family home and is dependent on an idealistic conception of mutually supportive membership based on geographical location.

The politically plausible argument for the closure of NHS and local authority long-stay provision is therefore challenged on the grounds of inaccurate definitions used to create a simplistic dualism: *Institutional care bad. Community care good* (Jack, 1998). Elderly people have, as a result, less choice.

The consequence of the transfer of elderly care first to social care and then to the private sector has been that residential homes are now required to provide for highly dependent and frail people, mainly elderly, although their experience was gained with younger, fit disabled groups (Redfern, 1998). Jones (1998) raises concern over a loss of expertise, built up since the early criticisms of institutional care within local authority care of the elderly, and the move to inappropriate private provision. The increased levels of need and dependency being met outside hospitals, both in residential and home care, it is argued, are falling on carers with little training and experience and with little control or support. Jack (1998) points out that the task of 'tending' has been devalued as personal care has become low-status manual work. The consequence for standards of care, when low status leads to low moral and sense of personal worth, seems likely to be an inevitable decline.

The belief that individual freedom consists exclusively of freedom from interference by the state – negative freedom – resulted in measures that sought to establish individuated rights rather than collective rights enforceable by virtue of membership in a particular community (Nettleton and Burrows, 1998). The individual as a consumer of health and social care was to be given the right of choice through the purchaser/provider split which established a quasi-market in healthcare, and through GP fundholding. Providers would be in competition with each other and league tables would ensure that GPs could choose on behalf of their patients, the consultants and hospitals that proved to be most effective (Harrison and Pollitt, 1994).

Social services were also given a purchaser role in respect of residential and home care services. Again, the individual, once need had been established and defined, was to have choice exercised through a professional, in this case a care manager. The choice is between parallel services, not whether a service should be funded. The professional gatekeeper, within the constraints of appeals systems, is the effective consumer (Paton, 1994).

Citizens' rights

Individuated rights assume that citizens are capable of and able to exercise them. Jones (1998) identifies the problem of families and elderly people who may not, under the stress of the moment, *be able to grasp regulations and official procedures*. One example, an elderly lady with no kin, she describes as *lost in a world where people assumed that she had a social competence she had never possessed and could not learn*.

The responsibility for obtaining their rights lies with the free citizen who can choose to exit (remove their custom), vote or to complain to the unsatisfactory provider. Thus the perceived paternalism of the welfare state is reduced or removed. However, when entrance to the system depends on influencing those in authority positions who are operating in a climate of increasing budget limitation and rationing, the social skill and status of the most vulnerable become an issue. The enabled citizen is an ideal whose reality may be quite limited, perhaps not only by age and health status but also by education and social class (Jones, 1998).

The argument that fundholding GPs might 'cream skim' patients least likely to be expensive (Glennerster et al., 1994) is one aspect of this concern. Cochrane (1998) argues that far from being enabled by consumer status in the welfare market, there exists a reduced emphasis on accountability that has resulted in *passive consumers receiving what is best for them* according to the accountants who are the only experts who are not challenged. Cochrane cites William Waldegrave while responsible for the creation of the Citizen's Charter, as stating that *democratic accountability was irrelevant to the operation of the local welfare state*. The quality of service, measurable above all by its economy, Cochrane argues, is the only politically correct standard applied and thus citizenship is devalued.

'Dis-welfare' for the elderly in a climate of consumerism and individual competitiveness may originate in misconceptions about the nature of community and family life in the 1990s. Mayo (1994) points out that the supportive community implied by care in the community is essentially a feminine phenomenon and the burden of caring has historically fallen to women. The economic necessity for women to work, failure of the benefits system to support working carers, increasing divorce and serial marriage, the geographical dispersal of families, and increasing numbers of the very old who have no surviving family are cited as flaws in the concept of community care (Mayo, 1994; Jones, 1998).

Individuated citizenship, incorporating notions of articulate, assertive people consciously seeking their own self-interest in competition with others in their relations with the welfare state, it may be argued, is inherently discriminatory against the less competitively placed in society. The subordinate position of social rights, compared with political and civil rights, by virtue of their lack of legal enforceability (Dean 1996), leaves those with the greatest dependency on the welfare state with the greatest need to compete effectively and be proactive in their own interests.

The rhetoric of freedom of the individual and responsive organisations, and the decentralisation of responsibility, through managerialisation, creation of NHS trusts and devolved budgets, coexist with tightening central control of overall public spending. Clarke and Newman (1998) describe the tensions between the 'centrifugal and centripetal' forces at work, which distance the centre from rationing at the individual and local level, the responsibility of trusts, managers or professionals, while ensuring that the rights of the consumer render decisions about provision more transparent and the budgetary imperative to ration becomes more insistent. Nettleton and Burrows (1998) discuss the individualisation process from the perspective of a late-modern culture of personal risk reduction, life-planning and self-development. They argue that there is an increasing requirement to make long-term life plans and lifestyle choices, and that this has in part come from political policies designed to de-emphasise state responsibility for individuals and to give simplistic digests of information such as league tables and audits to facilitate decision-making.

Choice becomes an imperative, and the choice of a healthy lifestyle and therefore freedom from illness and dependency, is an external mark of good citizenship. Nettleton and Burrows echo a point made by Dean (1996) that *when resources are rationed, those who exercise their 'rights' successfully may do so at the expense of others*. Nettleton and Burrows (1998) see the *marketisation of welfare* as inhibiting the ability of individuals to make altruistic choices and therefore to achieve a sense of citizenship.

Conclusion

The recurrent base note of this chapter has been conflicting policy values: altruism and self-interest, enablement and constraint, freedom of choice and control of choice available. Dean (1996), in his discussion of social rights, concluded that social rights have been seen as *unavoidably dependent on and subordinate to the imperative of economic productivity*, even by left-of-centre thinkers. This all-pervasive culture of materialism leaves the vulnerable elderly, and other disadvantaged groups in society, denied their social rights by virtue of the redefinition of citizenship in terms of competition. The emergent picture has been of elderly people manipulated as economic counters between budget-holding institutions; enshrined as consumers but allowed to choose only through rationing professionals, and publicly defined as a burden on society.

Chapter 5

Intermediate care: Implications for service users

Eileen Qubain

Introduction

This chapter will look at intermediate care, critically analyse the social and political factors which influence it, explore the way the service is organised, the impact on the service user and analyse how I identify networks and work effectively in complex situations.

The King's Fund (2002) defines intermediate care as a:

short term intervention to preserve the independence of a person who might otherwise be forced to go into hospital or a nursing home. It is an active and intense way of helping those who have suffered from illness or injury to GET THEIR LIVES BACK. It includes a wide range of activities such as physiotherapy, speech and language therapy and practical support for everyday living.

Intermediate care

Steiner (2001, page 433) describes intermediate care as a bridge between hospital and home for those who need a blend of medical and social support. A key component of intermediate care is rehabilitation, although the rehabilitation profession has resisted the word 'care' because it is suggestive of passivity and disempowerment (Steiner, 2001, page 38). Contrary to this, intermediate care services are supportive rather than directive; they should be delivered in a way that is person-centred, with support given in or near the person's home, or in a home-like setting. It is a bold move away from the usual model of care where the option of convalescence is seen as allowing time for the 'patient' to accept their increased weakness and disability.

Recent policy initiatives have placed 'promoting independence' as a central theme in health and social care: *Social care should be given in ways that promote independence* (DoH, 1998). Intermediate care is a core element of the government's programme for improving services for older people, a concept that allows us to step outside safe and known methods of practice. It is seen as a radical change in the way health and social services operate. The philosophy and principles underlining intermediate care are driven by the NHS Plan (DoH, 1999) and the *National Services Framework for Older People* (DoH, 2001b) outlining the importance of care that is meaningful and relevant to people. Bound up in this is the single assessment process which should lead to co-ordinated and effective assessments converging across health and social boundaries, with one central point of access providing an assessment of need that is relevant, and which promotes older people's independence and dignity.

Government policy

At the heart of healthcare there has always been the rhetoric of 'partnership' and 'inter-professional working' is one of the terms expressed in government policy (DoH, 1997, 1998). This teamwork demands role clarification and agreements on how to move forward. Inevitably there may be disagreements and differences of opinion but it seems to me that the ideology and principles behind these policies are nothing new; indeed most health and social care workers have always been committed to working in a way that is person-centred and promotes independence. It is these values that attracted workers to their professions in the first place. Stevenson (2003, page 20) described intermediate care as essentially old wine in new bottles. Back in 1968 Licht (1968) defined rehabilitation as *concern with the intrinsic worth and dignity of the individual*, while Sinclair and Dickinson (1998, page 63) broadened the meaning as a *process aiming to restore personal autonomy in those aspects of daily living considered most relevant by patients or service users, and their family carers*. This demonstrates that person-centredness and work with family and carers has always been on the agenda. What is now different is that the government has articulated and legitimised these in guidance and statute, which compel the system to allow for this ethos to be practised at grassroot levels, with support from managers.

There are debates about the drive behind the concept of intermediate care. Kirby (2000, page 8) suggests, *intermediate care is a new name designed to deal with an old problem – that of older patients staying in acute beds and causing winter crises*. The powerful voice of older people who will have considerable influence at election time may be a significant factor in the government's promotion of the status of older people, but this may be only one part of a very complex issue.

Skerrett (2000, page 64) sees social work as a social and political activity in which the welfare state is reflected. She takes this further by proposing that as social workers we cannot enable clients unless we are aware of the social context in which they live and how this is influenced by social policy. This view is supported by Brechin (2000, page 25), who asserts that grasping the policy context of cases is vital in enabling practitioners to work effectively. In direct opposition, Dunn (1985, page 17) puts forward a picture of neglect of the political dimension by many nurses and related disciplines when she argues, *politics is for others. Politics is a deviant activity in which no self-respecting professional should indulge*. It is important to look at the history of British social policy and grapple with this 'deviancy', acknowledging that *social work is the interaction between people and their environment* (Banks, 1995b, page 63).

With the introduction of the Beveridge Report (1942) came the promise of collective protection against the ills of want, unemployment, disease, squalor and ignorance (Adams, 2002, page 46). This welfare emphasis, which was to be universally available, was a distinct move away from the individualistic philosophy dominant in pre-war years based on a premise of the 'deserving and undeserving'. During the Conservative governments of Thatcher and Major, there was a return to free-market capitalism, which supports an individualistic approach where the strong survive. This was very much influenced by Hayek, who believed the concept of society to be a myth, a statement echoed by Margaret Thatcher, who felt that personal freedom should not be eroded by the state in terms of taxes or collective responsibility.

After Labour's rise to power in 1997, Blair attempted to establish a new consensus around issues such as welfare, employment and citizenship citing (1998) *equal value, opportunity for all, responsibility and obligation* as key themes in the 'Third Way'. In a Labour Party conference speech, Blair (2004) refers to a move away from the traditional welfare state and introduces a vision of an 'opportunity society' where the individual has both rights and responsibilities. He identifies the central values of his new direction to be equity, solidarity, and a society of mutual obligation. Interwoven in rhetoric about the Third Way there is a recurrent theme in references to 'responsibility, obligation, contracts and reciprocity' with an underlying ambition to *break the mould of the old passive benefits system* (DSS, 1998, page 24). Similarly, the Community Care Minister Stephen Ladyman (2004, page 44) criticises models of social care provision which *hold people in a culture of dependency*, citing choice, diversity and person-centredness as tenets of his 'bottom-up' vision for the future of social care.

In this vein the state is seen as an agency that informs and guides people to make wise decisions about their health, diet, education and employment, fostering and formulating personal projects while instilling a sense of mutuality and drive towards the common good. Jordan (2000, page 49) argues that there needs to be a presence and balance between individualism and collectivism for ethical social work practice, and it would seem that in his Third Way, Blair was attempting to balance these two elements. Achieving this balance is no easy feat and looking behind the rhetoric are shades of a return to 'deserving and undeserving'. Jordan (2000, page 13) paints a powerful picture of the safety nets constructed by the Beveridge reforms being replaced with a trampoline to 'bounce' people out of the benefits system into independence. But what happens to those who cannot bounce? Intermediate care, with a focus on rehabilitation, could be seen as an instrument to help people bounce out of dependency and as such it is given prominence and funding in health and social care.

But behind the door of this rhetoric there are major factors knocking hard on the government's agenda, which cannot be ignored. There is the tremendous influence of an ageing society, where between 1995 and 2025 the number of people over the age of 80 in England is set to increase by almost half, and the number of people over 90 will double (DoH, 2000). This coupled with the economic factors, and the cost of long-term care provision is significant and the government has had to look at ways of managing this.

I would argue that intermediate care is a robust vehicle to support and empower people, but its effectiveness is dependent on its definition and application. The question is:

Is the endeavour and bedrock of intermediate care, reinforced by the National Services Framework for Older People (DoH, 2001b), to motivate, empower and promote self-esteem, or is it a tool for bed management?

Interprofessional working

In my locality we have a wealth of intermediate care service, which provides intensive short-term support, and sees service users through a critical period by promoting independence and rehabilitation opportunity. These services can be located in a community unit, within a residential or nursing-home setting, or within a person's own home, and we consider that we are fairly wealthy in terms of the options available to us in our area. The impact of intermediate care within our wider hospital-based team has been a powerful one and there have been good interdisciplinary links developed over time. These have been extended and strengthened by the vehicle of intermediate care in which a high level of partnership is required. It has given a clearer definition of multidisciplinary working and improved understanding of the roles and values each team member has. We share not only a budget, but also expertise, knowledge, skills and responsibility, which has forced us to constantly articulate and reshape our shared aims and visions in each individual piece of work. It has also provided a forum for learning from each other, sharing experiences and disappointments, evaluating our successes or lack of it, and for our practices to suit the individual. We have learned that spending time together is key to improving our sense of belonging to the team.

We have experienced tensions and disagreements prompted by extreme pressure and limited resources, but by working closer together, we have found ways of resolving these. There are times when we begin to revert to the bitter question of whether this is a 'medical' or a 'social' problem, and time and energy are wasted on debating this. In truth, it is hard to unpick the threads and separate the two. Being in close proximity is crucial, and having regular meetings and reviews helps our steps to be co-ordinated, and makes working together infinitely easier. In the future I believe that these foundations could and must be taken further with opportunities for joint training, sharing away-days to look at specific health and social care issues, and reminding and updating our vision of what our service is.

The people who are referred to our service need support to 'get their lives back' when it feels as if part of it has been stolen by acute illness, disability, or an exacerbation of their chronic condition. On the whole, there is scope for incredible flexibility, and we look at a way forward together within the confines of the limitations placed on us by the harsh reality of eligibility criteria, stretched services and financial pressure. Where there have been 'clashes' we have worked hard at talking things through in a way that is both respectful and upholds the bonds we have worked so hard to develop. There is too much to lose, both for us as a team and for the people with whom we work, to jeopardise these relationships which determine the success or failure of our service. Hudson (1991, page 78) states, *It is clear that collaboration in social welfare has no qualities of spontaneous growth or self-perpetuation. Progress will only stem from the most vigorous commitments.*

As a social worker I find the concepts and rationale behind the ideas of intermediate care to be liberating both for the 'person' and the 'team' involved. I believe it invites us to adopt a social model of care, rather than slavery to traditional and narrow confines inherent in a medical model. Ryan and Thomas (1987, page 27) suggest, *Medical model thinking tends to support the status quo*. Intermediate care heartily dispels the myth that patients should be passive recipients of care. It has given control and power back to the person, making the patients 'director of their own care', as well as giving to nurses and other team members what Binnie and Titchen (1999) describe as *freedom to practice*. It questions the role of 'consultant' as the only expert, underlines the idea of client expertise in themselves, as well as elevating and nurturing the status of the 'team'. This idea of professional autonomy pulls us together, and invites us to practise in a way that suits the person and the context in which they live, rather than the organisation for which we work. I feel that our values and philosophies, now shaped and underpinned by intermediate care, should no longer be different. There is not the same struggle over finances and responsibility, although this remains a potentially explosive area. We have learned mutual respect for the different constraints of each discipline involved. We have struggled together over 'rights versus risks' issues in looking at promoting independence, balanced with safety. We have together shaped the way our team has evolved and because of tight timescales, there has been imperative for good and frequent communication.

Fennell et al. (1998, page 17) allude to *Unwarranted application of negative stereotypes to older people*. There has been a tendency for older people to be dismissed and have their humanity denied as they are often presented as useless and a burden. In countering this, Phillipson (1989, page 205) introduces 'interdependency', which he claims: *Provides recognition of help older people need from us, as well as rewards to be gained from giving this help. It also reminds us of skills possessed by older people and the resources these might provide for activities and campaigns within the community.*

Support networks

Secker et al. (2003, page 386) identify reciprocity as a main theme emerging in literature about independence and highlight the importance of creating and maximising opportunities for older people to engage in reciprocal networks of support. This is something that intermediate care can offer with opportunities to enable people to step back into their place and life in the community where they have a valuable contribution to make, if this is what they wish to do. An example of this has been working with someone who wanted very much to increase her mobility so that she could attend church on Sundays; another wanted to resume his place as chairperson for the Severn Valley Railway Association. Cresswell (1996, page 180) asks *what is social work if it is not the interlinking of systems, and the ways of working with them? Networking is essential to execute the principles of community care.*

In intermediate care the personal resources a service user has at their disposal is as crucial as the 'professional' networks we work within. These personal networks should act as a guide in looking at what wider support is needed and available. Middleton (1994, page 79) states that assessments should start with the hopes and aspirations of users and carers, rather than looking outside for answers, and dwelling on deficits and difficulties. Intermediate care with its emphasis on person-centred care should build on the individual's strengths and coping strategies, rather than undermining them. Sometimes through critical life events the networks people have are weakened, and intermediate care has a role in helping to strengthen them, by offering support, practical advice and assistance. Research has highlighted the importance of building on family cohesion and their internal organisation (Dale, 1996, page 31) and there are times when we have jumped in too quickly and offered support that does not fit in with the person's own network or system. Similarly, there have been times when we have failed to realise the struggle of family and carers and have assumed that they are able and prepared to continue caring, when it comes to light that this is not the case. These are errors made when we fail to adequately listen to people, and when the pressures of moving things on leads to us losing sight of the person and their carers.

Research shows (Green, 1996, page 382) that older people are less likely than other patients to be involved in joint decision-making with health professionals, and some studies find that they are not consulted at all (Minichiello, 2000, page 253). Paterson (2001, page 574) contends that the culture of the 'practitioner as expert' is deep-rooted and that accepting lay knowledge as being of equal value raises fundamental challenges for the way in which practitioners view themselves. The National Services Framework tackles this issue by stating a directive that age discrimination is rooted out, and that care should be person-centred. Intermediate care goes a long way to addressing the problem of 'people being done to' and demands that choice and decision-making are handed back to the person wherever possible. DoH (2001b) acknowledges that there must be a *major shift in culture and attitude … if disabled people and their families are to be engaged as experts.* In our area all notes are left at the service user's home, and they have access to read and add any information or reflections they have. This is a shared record of the aims and support in place to achieve these, with the ultimate ownership being with the service user. This has had an impact on service users, many who are puzzled and surprised that they can access their notes, and contribute to them. This does not eradicate hidden agendas altogether but goes a considerable way to inclusion and honest communication. Steiner (2001, page 434) identifies that the potential of intermediate care is uniting professionals in their efforts to listen to older patients, elicit patients' individual goals and provide the services that will empower older people to come as close to meeting these goals as is possible. This firmly places the 'patient' at the centre of any work done and so building a framework of support around the patients' networks and resources should be the natural starting point. Smale et al. (1993, page 116) recognise that *people are experts in themselves, their situations, relationships and needs.*

Quality of life

A central feature of intermediate care is that it acknowledges the links between the functional view of 'rehabilitation' and 'existential concerns' such as 'personal identity' and 'loss of self', often eroded through chronic ill health. There is a tendency to equate quality of life with functional ability only and look at activities of daily living and assess only practicalities of 'self-care' skills. A majority of our service users are older people and Steiner (2001, page 434) identifies that for elderly people it is quality of life, and not physical function, which is central, and it must be recognised that independence means something very different to each one of us.

Corbett (1989, page 153) states:

> *Real independence is nothing to do with cooking, cleaning, and dressing oneself. If you ask me what is my experience of being independent, I would not automatically think about self help skills but of being able to use my imagination to create fantasy, of enjoying music and drama, of relishing sensual pleasure and absorbing the natural life around me.*

Rehabilitation needs to be 'relevant' and meaningful to people and it should enable us to see that what works for one person in the 'healing process' does not necessarily work for another. Geelen and Soons (1996, page 69–77) refer to information being given to patients in a way that fits into their world and experience, acknowledging that metaphorical images intermeshed with areas of interest of the person can prove useful and powerful. They cite an example of a retired car mechanic with arthritis in his knee joints being given an explanation of his condition in which a comparison is made with poor shock-absorbers in a car. In order to be able to make these links and capitalise on the resources people have within them, time has to be invested in getting to know and understand the person, what matters to them, what they want to achieve and what motivates them. For some of the service users we have worked with they have indicated what really matters to them is getting out to the hairdressers or the bookmakers, rather than being able to stand in the kitchen and cook a meal. For some this is how life quality is measured, and indeed why should we impose our standards and ideals on another person, who has their own wealth of knowledge and their own pattern of life which they value and hold dear? Having this goal gives motivation and the will to participate in the rehabilitation process and intermediate care gives us opportunity to be creative and flexible in accommodating need as far as we are able.

However, over the time that intermediate care has developed in our area, the pressures of speedy hospital discharges have gathered momentum, and with the implementation of the Community Care (Delayed Discharges) Act 2003 there is an increased imperative to move people on. On personal reflection, I feel that there is less opportunity to work with existential concerns and that the drive is now to concentrate on the functional abilities of people to 'bounce them out' of an overstretched system. There remain windows for looking beyond this, but this appears to be dependent on the will, motivation and drive of the different intermediate care resources and the staff who manage them. This highlights the need for excellent multidisciplinary work with a shared vision and culture. Without this, the opportunities inherent in intermediate care are lost, and it is at serious risk of becoming *an antidote for the bed blocking crisis* (Wade and Lees, 2002, page 8).

The range of intermediate care services locally provides a plethora of choice and if used correctly, we have countless examples of people who have benefited greatly from support in these different circumstances. However, there are also examples when people are passed from one service to the other. One service user described feeling like a 'package' being passed around. In looking at staffing changes in the NHS, Williams (1992 in Biggs, page 153) asserts that there is *no longer cradle to grave, but from pillar to post*. With the introduction of different pockets of intermediate care services, this is a real issue for many elderly, vulnerable and bewildered service users who are passed from one resource to another.

Biggs (1993, page 153) states that service users often have considerable experience of relying on services that are organised around priorities other than their own, and this appears to be an increasing danger in intermediate care. This makes a nonsense of the idea of a 'seamless service' which is identified as an aim in service provision, and begs the question: for whose benefit are these services instituted?

There is also a drive towards ensuring that only the 'right type of person', who presents as being motivated, co-operative and able to benefit from what is on offer, receives intermediate care, rationing the stretched resources to ensure the most effective use of service. I understand that there is not a bottomless pot of money and that there needs to be some rationing. However, I also feel that behind this there are shades of the deserving and undeserving, with vulnerable people almost having to prove their worth in the rehabilitation arena, or have someone who will argue their case for them if they are unable. If they cannot be seen to 'fit into' what services are on offer, then people do not have those choices or opportunities. In this 'value for money culture', where there are targets to meet and beds to empty, there is decreasing drive to look at the emotional needs bound up in rehabilitation, and lost opportunities in a system whose rhetoric boasts helping people to 'get their lives back'.

Carers

Another major issue is the impact that intermediate care can have on carers. With the emphasis on providing support outside of the setting of the acute sector, and wherever possible within a person's own home, there is a danger that carers' needs can be overlooked in the assessment process. The Carers Recognition and Services Act 1995 has signalled the fact that carers should no longer be *the Cinderellas of social policy* (Twigg and Atkin, 1994, page 80), but there remains a tremendous pressure and expectation on carers to be a key part of the process, when this may not be what the carer wants. Traditionally, when the cared-for person has been admitted into hospital this is a time for the carer to have a break from the caring role. Intermediate care has the potential to work with carers in a positive way by looking at support networks that may help them in their role, and identify resources available to carers in their own right. It can allow opportunity for a carer's assessment to be done away from the frenzy of a hospital admission where many carers decline an assessment of their own needs. This can lead to emotional help, as well as some practical assistance and guidance. I have been able to do some carers' assessments within intermediate care which has opened up all sorts of support and has given the carer a wider access to the multidisciplinary team in addressing their concerns and worries. Within the acute setting this is not always possible.

Conclusion

On balance, my observation and experience of intermediate care has been positive, with people being freed from making permanent and life-changing decisions at a time of great crisis. The majority of cases referred to the intermediate care team are complex, and behind the initial contact reason, there are often many other chronic medical problems and underlying issues, which complicate the road to recovery. I have witnessed people regaining their confidence, dignity and place in their community where intermediate care has allowed flexibility in goal planning. As a team we have the opportunity to look at wider issues of discrimination, power and disadvantage, an area I feel that social workers are particularly tuned into. Thompson (1993, page 10) asserts that a social work practice that does not take account of oppression and discrimination cannot be seen as good practice. In this area I feel that we have something to offer our health colleagues as these issues are not discussed as widely in their training structures, and yet they are a foundation of social work training. Using the strengths and expertise of different team members assists in complex cases where there is a need for multiple skills, and different approaches to achieve a positive outcome. In cases where people have not benefited as they should, or have not had access to the services they should have, it seems mostly to have been the result of a loss of shared vision and purpose within the multidisciplinary team. This is often caused by a breakdown in communication and an overriding pressure to move people on. Critical analysis of work and self is crucial in working within an anti-oppressive framework. Hopson (1981, page 154) suggests *we are unable to help others if we do not know ourselves, our own strengths and weaknesses*. As a team, acknowledging and working with these issues is imperative in developing true partnership. Working in a climate of collaboration, co-operation and clear communication makes work more fulfilling and therefore staff morale increases, which cascades down to the service user. Nolan and his colleagues (Nolan, 1997; Davies et al., 1999; Nolan et al., 2001) suggest that staff are unlikely to be able to create an environment in which an older person feels significant, and that they matter, if they themselves do not feel valued. As a team we have noted how respect and value are infectious, and feedback from service users indicates that they do feel valued and listened to, and this in turn increases the possibility for positive recovery. We feel that the quality of the service we provide is heavily dependent on the quality of the relationships we develop.

Steiner (2001, page 434) refers to controversy around intermediate care and asserts that it is both a puzzle and a challenge. In managing this, tools such as theory, legislation, codes of practice, supervision and the opportunity for informal discussion with colleagues help me deal with difficulties presented. Casement (1985, page 136) suggests that developing an 'internal supervisor' allows one to stand outside one's self to monitor the complex processes and dynamics entailed in work. This is especially true in intermediate care where it is easy to get driven along, when sometimes the right thing to do is to 'slow things down' to allow us as a team to look at the whole picture. I hope that we can build on the positive foundation we have for intermediate care in our area and work with *the challenge to move beyond the rhetoric to make person centred care visible* (Nolan, 2000, page 49).

Chapter 6

To what extent is self-directed support actually self-directed by people with learning disabilities?

Jonathan Monk

Introduction

'Self-directed support' is the name given to the framework for transforming the social care system to one where people have much greater choice and control over the services they receive. The concept of self-directed support generally relates to a range of approaches and mechanisms to deliver more personalised outcomes for the people that use services, usually through the provision of personal budgets that allow them to design their own community care package and choose how they receive the support they need. In this way, self-directed support represents a major shift in the way services are traditionally organised, delivered and experienced by the people that require social care.

However, the starting point for self-directed support is not with services but with the individual themselves along with their family and community (Pitts et al., 2009, page 4). Indeed, self-directed support is underpinned by a strong philosophical value base that starts with the individual as a person with strengths and preferences who is *best placed to know what they need and how those needs can be best met* (Carr and Dittrich, 2008, page 3).

This chapter will consider the contextual evolution of self-directed support in England in order to analyse how the concept has been shaped and introduced as part of the current programme for social care transformation. It would appear that there is a whole new framework of concepts, processes and mechanisms emerging within the language of self-directed support. This chapter will seek to clarify the main terms and concepts associated with self-directed support. The chapter will then go on to consider the key features of self-directed support and will evaluate its impact on both a macro and micro level, in order to consider the implications for the individual, their family and communities. The chapter will explore the implications for social work practice and for wider public service provision for people with learning disabilities, examining the rhetoric of increased choice and control for individuals with the realities in practice.

The chapter will then go on to consider some of the mechanisms and models of practice emerging to illustrate how self-directed support can assist people with learning disabilities to really be involved in decision-making in order to exercise increased choice and control over their lives.

The evolution of self-directed support in England

Social care services have been organised and delivered in multiple ways, some of which can be seen to be more personalised than others. Priestley (1999, page 168) argues that unless the inputs, processes and outputs of services enable people to make real changes in their lives, *they are of little value*. On this basis, the examination of self-directed support in England must also focus on outcomes rather than processes and systems. Indeed, the concept of 'outcomes' is now routinely applied in any analysis of self-directed support (CSIP, 2007, page 1; Leadbeater et al., 2008).

The set of outcomes envisaged by the community care policy and legislation of the early 1990s were, broadly speaking, those associated with the concept of normalisation; that is, services that enable people to live as ordinary and normal a life a possible. Clearly, there are many limitations to this approach, least of which being the value-laden and subjective nature of what is 'normal', the implied sense of conformity and question of *whose norms should be employed as the 'gold standard'*? (Priestley, 1999, page 168). However, it can be argued that the outcomes associated with self-directed support, such as integration, inclusion, involvement and empowerment, have their origins in normalisation theory.

The emergence of self-directed support can be seen to have its roots in the philosophy of independent living and the social model of disability (Spandler, 2004, page 188). As such, Priestley (1999, page 196) suggests that the independent living movement has required disabled people *to demonstrate that they can be effectively engaged, not only as consumers but as the producers of welfare*. To this end, the disability movement argued that in order to achieve true independent living, there had to be emphasis on disabled people securing the resources with which they might manage their own affairs (Priestley, 1999, page 99).

The emphasis of the community care legislation was on local authority management of resources and provision of services. Indeed, there remained the specific prohibition of local authorities making cash payments in lieu of providing community care services, as originally set out in the 1948 National Assistance Act (Monk, 2006, page 57). Therefore, the scope for people to truly shape and control their own support arrangements remained extremely limited.

It can be argued that the most significant development in the early inception of self-directed support was the establishment of the Independent Living Fund (ILF) in 1988

(Priestley, 1999, page 201). Using funding from central government, ILF was established with the intention to support disabled people of working age to remain in their own homes and communities through cash payments (up to a weekly maximum). In November 1992, the ILF was closed to new applicants and replaced by two new funds: the Independent Living (Continuation) Fund for existing claimants, and the Independent Living (1993) Fund for new claimants, both operating different award criteria and conditions. The impact on the evolution of self-directed support of ILF as the pioneer for cash payments and personal care budgets cannot be underestimated, with the number of people benefiting from the fund totalling over 21,500 people as at September 2009 (ILF, 2009).

However, despite the success of ILF in testing individualised funding initiatives, it was the only example of such arrangements and as such, was administered by central, rather than local, government. In the UK, the pressure for direct payments administered by the local authority continued. The main source of such pressure came from organisations of disabled people who were dissatisfied with the range and responsiveness of services, and in particular, the inadequacy, inflexibility and insensitivity to individual needs along with the levels of bureaucracy disabled people were experiencing (Spandler, 2004, page 188). As a result of this pressure, a small number of local authorities gave financial grants to voluntary organisations to administer third-party 'indirect payments' arrangements.

The introduction of direct payments initially received cautious support from the serving Conservative government. Pearson (2000, page 461) suggests that the government were concerned with *cost efficiency and accountability of public spending*, alongside concerns about the potential demand for the scheme.

The Community Care (Direct Payments) Act 1996 gave local authorities the power to make Direct Payments. However, this power applied only to adults below the age of 65 years. It wasn't until February 2000 that the power to make direct payments was eventually extended to older people, under the Labour government. However, the 1996 Act provided only a discretionary power to local authorities. This was not mandatory and there was no guarantee of local availability.

The 1996 legislation also stated that potential users must consent to receiving a direct payment. The associated guidance affirmed that people should also be willing and able to manage direct payments. As a result, many people with learning disabilities were deemed to be ineligible. As such, a number of local authorities developed blanket policies that specifically excluded people with learning disabilities from receiving direct payments. However, since 2003, local authorities now have a duty to make direct payments to all people who are assessed as being eligible for community care support (with the exception of long-term residential care) and who consent to receiving this support in the form of a direct payment (Dow, 2004, page 20).

Indeed, new regulations introduced in November 2009 extended the duty to make direct payments even further to include people who lack capacity to consent. As a result, local authorities must offer direct payments to all eligible adults and the payment can now be made to a 'willing and appropriate suitable person', such as a family member or friend, who will receive and manage the payments on behalf of the person who lacks capacity (DoH, 2009d, page 1). These extensions to the legislative and regulatory framework are seen to be critical to giving people the opportunity to control the resources allocated to their support.

However, take-up of direct payments has been variable across local authorities and service user groups and still remains relatively low. Indeed, in 2008/09, 86,000 adults were in receipt of direct payments with spend equating to only 4 per cent of the overall gross current expenditure on social care in England (CQC, 2010, page 15). In 2008, according to CSCI (2008, page 52), approximately 9,000 adults with learning disabilities (15–65) were in receipt of direct payments. The barriers to direct payments for people with learning disabilities have been the area of considerable analysis in recent years and are discussed in more detail elsewhere (Joseph Rowntree Foundation, 1999; CSCI, 2004; Monk, 2006).

Therefore, despite high-profile campaigns (such as the CSIP Social Care Programme's Increasing the Uptake of Direct Payments programme in 2006) and considerable investment from both local and central government (including £4.5 million allocated to 44 voluntary and community-sector organisations as part of the Department of Health Direct Payments Development Fund, 2003–2005), the number of people directing their own support through direct payments remains *disappointingly low* (CSCI, 2004, page 5).

It is widely argued that 'whole system change' is required in order to achieve the outcomes of choice, control and personalisation and that this was not possible under the current model for social care (Hall and Newman, 2008, page 2).

In 2003, six local authorities, through the In Control project, undertook to redesign the way the social care system worked. In Control was set up as a partnership initiated by the Valuing People Support Team, Mencap, local authorities and independent organisations, in order to examine the changes required to create a system of self-directed support that achieves improved outcomes for the people using social care. The project led to the creation of the first Individual Budget for a young man with learning disabilities, and managed by his mother (Tomlinson, 2006). By 2007, In Control had over 90 local authority members developing self-directed support in their localities and at the end of 2008, there were approximately 10,000 people in receipt of Individual Budgets (In Control, 2009). The key features, principles and outcomes of the In Control project will be examined in more detail at a later stage in this chapter.

Influenced by the learning and success of the In Control project, in 2005 the Prime Minister's Strategy Unit published *Improving the Life Chances of Disabled People,* which built on the concept of self-directed support and in particular the use of Individual Budgets to give people the optimum amount of choice and control over their support while countering some people's fears about becoming employers through direct payments. This was consolidated by the focus on Individual Budgets as part of the government's Green Paper *Independence, Well-Being and Choice* (DoH, 2005b) and the *Our Health, Our Care, Our Say: A new direction in community services* White Paper (DoH, 2006a).

In response, the Prime Minister requested that the Department of Health commissioned a pilot for Individual Budgets working alongside the Department of Work and Pensions and the then Office of the Deputy Prime Minister (now the Department of Communities and Local Government). The pilot worked across 13 local authority areas for a period of two years. In October 2008, the Individual Budgets Evaluation Network (IBSEN) published its findings on the pilot.

In December 2007, the cross-government agency concordat *Putting People First: A Shared Vision and Commitment to the Transformation of Adult Social Care* was published, setting out the vision to transform public services to create a more personalised care service where personal budgets and self-directed support would *become the norm* (Community Care, 2007, page 1). It can be argued that *Putting People First* cemented this concept of personalisation within public policy as the means to offer people *practical ways to live their lives rather than receive a service* (Routledge, 2008, cited in Community Care, 2009, page 1).

Funded through a ring-fenced grant of £520 million over three years, the concordat set out the principles by which local authorities, the NHS, voluntary-sector and private providers would work together. The concordat outlined plans to enhance information, advice and brokerage services and to encourage self-assessment. The vision also sets out a personalised system that focuses on prevention, early intervention and improved access to universal services. In this vision, personalisation is seen as much more than personal budgets, direct payments and self-directed support. However, they are key elements of the agenda. Indeed, cited in Community Care (2007, page 1), Health Secretary Alan Johnson stated that *our commitment that the majority of social care funding will be controlled by individuals, through personal budgets, represents a radical transfer of power from the state to the public. Everyone ... has the right to self-determination.*

In the context of the lives of people with learning disabilities, the policy commitment to personalisation was consolidated with the publication of *Valuing People Now: A new three-year strategy for people with learning disabilities* (DoH, 2009b) in January 2009. For people with learning disabilities and their families, *Valuing People Now* views personalisation as the means to secure improved outcomes in terms of social inclusion, empowerment and equality (DoH, 2009b, page 6). As such, the strategy sets out an expectation that more people should direct their own support arrangements and that the personalisation agenda must include and benefit people with learning disabilities and their carers.

The strategy builds on that set out in the original Valuing People agenda in 2001. That is, *that people with learning disability are people first with the right to lead their lives like any others, with the same opportunities and responsibilities* (DoH, 2009b, page 2). The notions of rights and responsibilities are key principles of self-directed support and will be explored more thoroughly in the next part of this chapter.

The key principles of self-directed support

It is argued that the overarching principle for the development of self-directed support is the desire to move to a system of social care where people have the ability to take greater control of their lives and the services they receive, enabling them to make the decisions and manage their own risks (CSIP, 2007, page 2).

However, it can be argued that the Labour government's overwhelming support for personalisation, particularly represented by mechanisms such as direct payments and personal budgets, is evidence of how Tony Blair's *Third Way* programme for public services has progressed (Jordan, 2001, page 528). The Third Way approach to welfare is to view people as 'consumer citizens' whereby people have a right to expect high-quality, person-centred and individualised services based on choice, freedom and self-direction. Indeed, the notion of rights and entitlements is strongly embedded within discourse relating to self-directed support. In Control (cited in *CareKnowledge*, 2008, page 4) set out a number of fundamental rights upon which self-directed support is based.

- The right to independent living.

- The right to an individual budget whereby the person is entitled to ongoing paid support as part of their life and should be able to decide how the money that pays for that help is used.

- The right to self-determination where decision-making is made as close to the person as possible, reflecting their own interests, preferences and aspirations.

- The right to accessibility in a system that has clear and transparent rules.

- The right to flexible funding where people are free to spend their funds in the way that makes sense to them and without unnecessary restrictions

In practice, self-directed support implies that people should not only be able to define their own needs, through a system of self-assessment, but also have the right to decide how those needs are met. However, alongside such rights to choice and control, there is increased emphasis on responsibility, accountability, participation and obligation (Jordan, 2001, page 529).

Indeed, the principle of citizenship is the central idea of the In Control model of self-directed support (Duffy, 2003, page 1). Duffy (page 2) suggests that citizenship is *the word we use to describe what it is to be recognised by other people as an individual who is a full member of the community … [and] provides us the opportunity to find out, on our own or with others, what we want to do with our lives*. According to Duffy (p.1), there are six keys to citizenship on which self-directed support is founded.

1 Self-determination, the authority to control our own life and to be able to get help from other people to achieve self-determination.

2 Direction, a purpose, plan or idea of what we want to achieve.

3 Money, to live and to control our own life.

4 A home, a place that is our own, a base for our life.

5 Support, to help to do the things that we need help to achieve.

6 A community life, an active engagement in the life of the community and the development of our own network of relationships.

On this basis, it can be argued that self-directed support originates at least in part from social work values (Carr and Dittrich, 2008, page 8). A core component of social work practice has always involved putting the individual first and values dignity and respect for people. There are clear links with the social work approach to self-determination as the recognition of the right of people to freedom in making their own choices and decisions that impact on their lives (Banks, 1995a, page 26). Indeed, if social work practice is intended to promote people's rights to choice and assist them to increase control of and improve the quality of their lives, self-directed support can be seen as a mechanism to do just that.

However, there is another side to this approach to self-directed support as a means of securing active citizenship for people who use social care services. That is the increased emphasis on responsibility for individuals and what many critics of self-directed support view as *transferring management responsibility from services to the individual service user or family carers* (Anonymous Family Carer, 2008, page 14). This transfer of responsibilities, with people effectively becoming their own care managers, does have implications for approaches to capacity and consent. This has significant implications for the extent to which self-directed support for people with complex needs is actually self-directed and will be discussed later in this chapter.

Duffy's (2003, page 1) approach to citizenship as a key principle of self-directed support explicitly includes the notion of 'social capital'. The emphasis is on community life and community engagement, with the development of networks based on trust, respect, support and participation. In this context, self-directed support can be seen to reflect social capital as *the potential of communities to improve the well-being of their members through the synergy of associates, mutual trust, sense of community and collective action* (Nelson and Prilleltensky, 2005, page 95). Examples of how self-directed support is increasing the social capital of people with learning disabilities is evident in people increasingly engaging in voluntary work; citizen advocacy; working on neighbourhood projects; and the emergence of service-user-led micro-enterprises. This is the notion of people with learning disabilities being visible as active participants in their local communities and having what is often described as *community presence* (O'Brien, 1987, cited in Harris, 2000, page 1). As a result of this increased social capital, people gain personal skills and confidence. Also, other people's perception of them is likely to change, where people are seen as active participants that can make a contribution.

As a result of using self-directed support to increase social capital and thus exercise their citizenship rights, people are also more likely to be able to access what are described in social policy as 'universal services'. These are the mainstream public, and in many cases, private services that are open to the community, such as housing, transport, leisure and education services. All components of the government's vision of a personalised social care system (as set out in *Putting People First*, DoH, 2008) and critical ingredients to making the *Valuing People Now* (DoH, 2009b) strategy a reality in the lives of people with learning disabilities. Improved access to having their own bank account is also perceived to be tangible evidence of increased citizenship rights for people with learning disabilities (Valios and Ahmed, 2006, page 27).

Social capital relates to another principle that is routinely used in relation to self-directed support: 'co-production' (Carr and Dittrich, 2008, page 11). This is relatively recent terminology that is emerging in welfare discourse and is used to refer to direct participation and community involvement in the development and delivery of social care services. Leadbeater et al. (2008, page 11) suggest that as people become direct participants in service planning, commissioning and provision both on a macro level (through user involvement in service design, commissioning and review) and on a micro level (as individual commissioners through direct payments and personal budget arrangements), they become co-producers of services rather than passive recipients of care. This in turn *changes people's attitudes to themselves and their role in the service* (Leadbeater et al., 2008, page 11). Indeed, the development of self-directed support has also seen the growth in profile and status of *experts by experience* (Carr and Dittrich, 2008, page 19). People with experience of using social care services or as informal carers are increasingly embracing self-directed support to forge opportunities for themselves to contribute to local authority transformation programmes as consultants. There is compelling evidence to suggest that the most successful programmes have included this type of co-production (Pitts et al., 2009).

It is also widely argued that improved outcomes for the individual in relation to increased confidence, self-esteem and energy levels can all be evidenced alongside reduced feelings of isolation, depression and dependence. Indeed, a key principle of self-directed support is for services to promote independence for the people that use them rather than fostering dependence (CSIP, 2007, page 3).

The features of self-directed support

As we have seen, a system self-directed support is designed to give the person and their family as much control of their support as possible. Leadbeater et al. (2008, page 27) suggest that there are a number of key features of self-directed support, which include the following.

- Devolve personal budgets to be as close to people as possible.

- Enable them to make plans how to use the money to create solutions for them that also deliver value for money.

- Allow people to use their budgets to commission services in line with these plans.

- Allow the plans to be modified by learning and changes in circumstances.

- Keep an overview of how well the plans perform to guard against undue risk.

As is evident throughout this process, a key feature of self-directed support is the change in relationship between professionals and the people that use services. In the traditional approach, professionals assess need and measure this against access criteria based on entitlement and eligibility. Professionals will then plan, arrange and provide services and will be responsible for evaluating the outcomes on the person's behalf. In this way, the professional role is often perceived as the 'gatekeeper and rationer' of resources and ultimately holds the power (CSIP, 2007, page 3). Leadbeater et al. (2008, page 11) suggest that under self-directed support, professionals retain an overview of quality and outcomes but they *become more like advisers, counsellors and brokers, guiding people to make better choices for themselves*. In this way, self-directed support can be seen to have a better fit with the traditional role and skills associated with social work as opposed to care management. Indeed, Carr and Dittrich (2008, page 17) suggest that under self-directed support, social workers could use their skills to fulfil *more creative, person centred roles*.

With these key features at the centre of the model, In Control (cited in Pitts et al., 2009, page 5) developed a seven-step process for self-directed support. The emerging tools and features of self-directed support are discussed under these steps.

Step 1: Setting the budget

The individual needs to be aware of how much money is available to them and the outcomes it must be used to achieve in order to develop a support plan. Pitts et al. (2009) state that to do this, the local authority should have a resource allocation system (RAS). The RAS takes the form of a self-assessment questionnaire that advises people, as early in the process as possible, as to the amount of funding available to them and what it should be used to achieve. A fundamental feature of self-directed support is that the resources are allocated up front so that people can plan how to use them.

Step 2: Planning the support

Based on the resources available, people draw up a support plan rather than having to accept a care plan devised by the care manager. The support plan should describe what that support will look like and what it will achieve. The plan will set out what is important to the person and what they want to achieve in their life. It should explain how the person will use their budget to make the changes they want in their lives. It is argued that support planning enables people to think of flexible and innovative ways of meeting their support needs (Leadbeater et al., 2008, page 25).

CSIP (2007, page 4) suggests that support planning encourages people to build on 'natural resources' that exist already in their lives, such as their own gifts and interests, what is available in their community, and the roles that their friends and family may want to have in supporting them, in addition to the support they will need to buy from outside of these networks. In this way, self-directed support can be seen to replicate the features of person-centred approaches and person-centred planning.

Like person-centred planning, it is recognised that people will need different kinds of help with support planning and a 'one size-fits all' approach will not be an effective way of developing the plan. Some people will feel confident to work with their families and network to produce a plan. However, other people will need a more practical approach and facilitation.

Again in direct comparison with person-centred planning, one of the criticisms of self-directed support is that it leads people to develop unrealistic support plans that operate outside of local authority eligibility criteria and financial resources. However, Leadbeater et al. (2008, page 25) enter into this debate by stating that *a support plan is not a wish list. Each support plan must specify how it will meet government policy objectives to keep a person healthy, safe and well.* Despite the rhetoric of fair and transparent allocation of resources, there is a counter-argument to suggest that self-directed support does not reconcile the issue of equitable distribution of resources and indeed, can be seen to *maximise inequality of outcome* (Fyson, 2009, page 5).

Step 3: Agreeing the plan

This question of distribution of resources brings us to the next step of the self-directed support process: agreeing the plan. The proposed plan must be signed off by the local authority. It is argued that this part of the process provides the checks and balances for the local authority to confirm the budget, check that the support plan is safe and that appropriate risk-taking is considered and agreed (Pitts et al., 2009, page 5).

Step 4: Organising the money

Once the resources and the plan are agreed, the person can decide how the budget is deployed. There are a number of options for how they can organise and deploy their personal budget, from taking the funding as a direct payment to asking the local authority to arrange and commission the support services on the person's behalf – this is set out and analysed in more detail elsewhere (Worcestershire County Council, 2009).

The level of responsibility and involvement for the person in organising the money will depend on how they choose to deploy the resources. Again, we must be clear that individualised funding arrangements do not necessarily involve the person taking the money as a direct payment and a range of other mechanisms, such as individual service funds, can be set up.

Step 5: Organising the support

Depending on how the person chooses to organise the money (in step 4), the delivery of support services can now be arranged. The key features here are that the person is in control of deciding how the resources are spent and that they can use their budget flexibly to achieve the outcomes agreed in the support plan. Typically, this part of the process is likely to involve such activities as commissioning a service; using a local authority service (the cost of which will be deducted from their overall budget); recruiting and employing personal assistants; or purchasing equipment.

Step 6: Living life

The next feature of this process according to In Control (cited in Pitts et al., 2009, page 5) is for people to *live life, in that when people are supported in ways and at times that are right for them, it is possible to live a full and active life*. The outcomes of self-directed support for people with learning disabilities and the potential to live a full and active life will be analysed in more detail later in this chapter.

Step 7: Review and learn

Under self-directed support arrangements, the local authority retains a statutory responsibility to monitor and review how well the plan has worked and the effectiveness of how the resources have been deployed. The review should be seen as an opportunity to learn and change the support plan to more effectively achieve the outcomes. However, the successful evaluation of outcomes is dependent on the clarity of objectives set out at the support planning stage (McDonald, 1999, page 86).

There are some fundamental questions that should be asked as part of the review and learning stage of the process: how involved was the person in developing the support plan? To what extent did they express their needs, preferences and the changes they would like to make in their lives? How involved were they in decision-making throughout the whole of the self-directed support process? How could the approach be enhanced to increase self-determination, citizenship and social capital? These questions are critical when considering the impact that self-directed support can have on the lives of people with learning disabilities. The next part of this chapter will seek to examine some of the key issues in relation to these questions and will set out some of the approaches and tools to support effective self-directed support for people with learning disabilities.

Does self-directed support achieve improved outcomes for people with learning disabilities?

This chapter has set out how self-directed support has evolved through policy and legislation with clear ethical and value principles based on rights and responsibilities operating alongside concepts of independent living, participation, control, choice and empowerment. We have seen how the self-directed support system has been developed with the ethos to give people more control and help to *achieve better lives and build stronger communities* (Duffy, cited in Pitts et al., 2009, page 2).

However, the question remains as to the extent of how self-directed support is actually self-directed by people with learning disabilities themselves, and does it achieve improved outcomes in practice?

There is compelling evidence from a range of sources to illustrate the improved outcomes and real changes that people have been able to achieve in their lives as a result of self-directed support (Valios and Ahmed, 2006; In Control, 2008; Pitts et al., 2009). Indeed, the evaluation and learning report of the second phase of In Control (2008) provides a considerable evidence base of the potential for improved outcomes. In the study, 196 people using self-directed support across 17 local authorities in England were involved in the evaluation and were asked about their experiences and to judge whether their lives had improved in relation to a number of dimensions. More than half (58 per cent) of the participants were people with learning disabilities although the findings were consistent across user groups. It should be noted that this is the largest collection of data of this type thus far and offers a snapshot of the impact of self-directed support on the lives of people with learning disabilities. Despite some limitations in the data (which were fully acknowledged by In Control in the 2008 report) and the challenges of scaling up self-directed support to a wider and larger population and the impact over a longer period of time, the report sets out some important messages (Henwood, 2008).

In summary, the following outcomes were reported through the evaluation.

- Almost all of the participants (97 per cent) reported that they had control over how their personal budget was spent.

- A large proportion (91 per cent) of participants indicated that they understood and were involved in deciding what they wanted to achieve through self-directed support.

- A high proportion (82 per cent) of participants reported that by using self-directed support they had made changes to previous support arrangements.

- Three-quarters (76 per cent) of the participants reported improvements in relation to quality of life since using self-directed support.

- Increased choice and control was experienced by 72 per cent of participants

- Improved community participation was experienced by 64 per cent of participants.

- Almost half of the participants (47 per cent) reported improvements in their general health and well-being since using self-directed support.

- More than half (55 per cent) of participants reported that they were more able to spend time with people they liked through using self-directed support.

- More than a quarter (29 per cent) of participants reported to feeling more safe and secure at home since using self-directed support, with 71 per cent of people reporting no change.

- More than a half (59 per cent) of participants reported a sense of improved personal dignity in their lives.

- A considerable minority (36 per cent) of participants indicated that their sense of economic well-being had improved.

- Only a small minority (about 5 per cent) of participants felt that their lives had got worse in any regard since using self-directed support.

The arrangements under self-directed support were also generally seen to be more cost-effective and better value for money than the services the person had received previously. The economic case for self-directed support has been widely analysed elsewhere (In Control, 2008; Leadbeater et al., 2008, page 35) and will not be discussed in this chapter. However, there has been some criticism that the government support for self-directed care is due to the perception that it is an acceptable way of reducing public expenditure (Fyson, 2009, page 4).

This evaluation sets out a clear indication that the majority of people using self-directed support believe it has had a positive outcome to many aspects of their lives. These findings are mirrored throughout similar studies of specific self-directed support projects and initiatives across the country (Worcestershire County Council, 2009; London Borough of Richmond, 2010; and others). As a result, Leadbeater et al. (2008, Page 33) suggest that *having the power to design one's own plan enables people to think more creatively about what services they want – and what they want to achieve in life*.

Much prominence is given to the provision of individualised funding arrangements. However, individualised funding provides the means by which the person can control their own support but will not on its own guarantee that the person will be able to direct their own support (Duffy, 2004, page 11). In this context, individualised funding arrangements are only a means to the end and not the end itself.

Clearly an important part of the lives of people with learning disabilities is their families. It can be argued that family members are often more involved in the lives of adults with learning disabilities particularly, in relation to liaising with services, managing and administering the person's affairs and advocating and representing the person's needs and views (Shearn and Todd, 1997, cited in Williams et al, 2003, page 221). As such, it is likely that self-directed support can only increase the involvement and responsibilities for family members (Anonymous Family Carer, 2008).

Williams et al. (2003, page 221) pose the question of whether there is a potential 'conflict of interest' for family members in relation to supporting the person they care for to direct their own support arrangements. Concerns relating to family members exerting control over the individual or inappropriately influencing the person's views or desired outcomes are all potential risks within the self-directed care model. The role of family members as advocates and their involvement in helping the person to direct their own support, choose and employ personal assistants and manage the paperwork and other money matters can all be perceived to be ways in which a family member could exert control over the person and their arrangements. Indeed, Williams et al. (2003, page 223) suggest that under such arrangements, family members can have *far too much power [that] could put the person back under their parent's control*. Conversely, it can also be argued that it is family members that know the person best and as such are best placed to support the person to develop their support plan and organise their support. How this process is approached is critical to ensuring that the person has as much opportunity as possible. This chapter will later explore some tools and approaches to maximise the person's involvement and to give them the opportunity to decide themselves how to involve their family members in a structured and productive way.

There is also a perception that self-directed support will inevitably increase levels of vulnerability and potential for exploitation and abuse for people with learning disabilities (Fyson, 2009, page 5). It is argued that individualised funding arrangements, particularly direct payments, will increase risk of financial abuse (Anonymous Family Carer, 2008, page 20). Other safeguarding issues relate to concerns about the employment of suitable support staff, and in particular the recruitment of personal assistants and the supervision of lone workers. There are also concerns about the level of power and control paid carers can exert so that effectively they are directing the support rather than the person themselves.

There are also concerns in relation to the community participation aspect of self-directed support. It is assumed that people with learning disabilities will be more exposed to other members of their local community who could be perceived as 'non-regulated', and as such, could make them more vulnerable to *befriending by abusers* (Fyson, 2009, page 5). Indeed, people may be more exposed to potential for abuse, harassment or exploitation and hate crime in local communities and this continues to be a significant problem for people with learning disabilities (DoH, 2009b, page 79). However, a positive risk-acceptance approach would counter these concerns by arguing that risk is an inevitable part of everyday life and as such, should be encouraged where it increases choice, control, independence and self-determination (DoH, 2007). Indeed, DoH (2007) acknowledges that avoiding and managing risk out of a person's life will inevitably inhibit their personal freedoms, choices and opportunities to live a self-directed life. In reality, some risks cannot be completely removed or managed, however much support the person has.

This approach to positive risk-taking and acceptance is seen as fundamental to the implementation of self-directed support in social care (DoH, 2007, page 52). However, it can also be seen as a major barrier to support being truly self-directed for people with learning disabilities, specifically where a care manager or family member is particularly concerned about potential risks.

In response, DoH (2007, page 49) has devised a supported decision tool to guide and record the discussion when a person's choices involve an element of risk. Supporting people to consider risk and be involved in risk decision-making is essential as part of this process. This should involve gathering information; identifying and framing what the actual and real risks in the situation are; through to weighing up the risk factors and exchanging ideas and solutions to minimise and reduce risks. The person and their support network should be central to the decision-making around risk, including deciding on a particular course of action and putting measures in place to promote self-directed support and minimise any negative consequences of risk.

This chapter has already alluded to some of the tensions for capacity and consent within the context of self-directed support. In this context, capacity is taken to mean that people are able to make decisions for themselves. It is clear from the implementation of the Mental Capacity Act 2005 that capacity should be approached on an individual basis and that people should be given appropriate information (in a format that is meaningful and accessible to them) with as much support as is needed to help them express themselves and make decisions. Indeed, supported decision-making should maximise use of enhanced communication methods such as the use of pictures, videos and objects of reference to support the person to express choices and preferences and to make decisions and understand the options available to them. The 2005 Act itself sets out some key principles that are relevant and likely to impact on decision-making for people with learning disabilities.

- People must be assumed to have capacity unless it is established that they do not.

- Capacity is decision-specific – people will have capacity to make some decisions in their lives but not others.

- Where a person is deemed to not have capacity, or where their lack of capacity is temporary, they may still be able to express some clear choices and decisions.

- People should not be deemed as incapable of making a decision because their decision may seem unwise.

- Before taking a particular course of action or making a decision, consideration should always be given as to whether the outcome could be achieved in a less restrictive way.

These principles should be embedded within successful person-centred planning, which in turn is itself an effective tool to maximise self-directed support for people with learning disabilities. Firstly, it is important to identify the key people in the person's life. These will be the people that know the person best; are trusted by the person; and who can generate ideas to go into the plan. The person may want to establish a circle of support. This is a group of people who meet together on a regular basis to support a person to express their choices and identify their outcomes and can assist them to make decisions that affect their lives. The members of the circle, which may include family, friends, neighbours, or other community members, are involved because they admire and care enough about the person to give their time and expertise to help the person to work towards their desired outcomes (Monk, 2006, page 67). These arrangements can also be formalised into an Independent Living Trust or a Microboard. Such arrangements are particularly helpful as a means of ensuring that people other than family members are involved and thus *sharing responsibility as well as power* (Williams et al., 2003, page 226). These types of arrangements can also be helpful as a means of contingency planning to identify the ongoing assistance a person may need to direct their own support in the future, as and when family members may not be able to support the person. Access to a range of advocacy support is also critical to ensuring that people are able to make effective decisions and self-direct their own support arrangements (Duffy, 2004, page 12). This should include the local availability of an independent citizen and self-advocacy.

Duffy (2003, page 46) sets out a number of practical tools and approaches that can be used to ensure that the person is fully involved in planning and decision-making. Planning Alternative Tomorrows with Hope (PATH) is a planning tool based on the work of O'Brien, Forrest and Pierpoint in Canada. It is a creative and visual process that uses graphics and colours to help people identify the changes and direction they would like their lives to follow. It enables people to consider their aspirations and dreams and is effective at capturing people's imagination. It is also seen as a fun process that enables people to set goals and to agree specific steps needed to achieve the person's outcomes. However, it is not an effective problem-solving tool and for some people, the notion of *thinking about their dreams can be too threatening* (Duffy, 2003, page 46). Making Action Plans (MAPS); Essential Lifestyle Planning (ELP); Life Building; and Personal Futures Planning (PFP) are all useful tools to engage the person in the planning and self-directed support process (Circles Network, 2008).

However, person-centred planning as a tool to facilitate self-directed support has some limitations. Person-centred planning should be proportionate and tailored to the specific changes a person wants to make in their lives – small or simple decisions may not require a full PATH or ELP approach. Indeed it would be inappropriate and inconsistent with the principles of self-directed support to apply a 'one-size-fits-all' approach to support planning.

Person-centred planning and self-directed support also has significant resource implications (CSCI et al., 2009, page 17). For instance, the use of specialist planning tools and the extra time it will take to prepare a person-centred support plan compared with the traditional care planning associated with the care management approach.

In their review of support for people with learning disabilities and complex needs, the Commission for Social Care Inspection, Healthcare Commission and Mental Health Act Commission (2009, page 16) found that few people were benefiting from person-centred planning, with even fewer people directing their own support through personal budgets or direct payments. The review set out that people with complex needs had 'severely restricted' choices and even fewer opportunities for employment or co-production. Indeed, it could be argued that people with complex needs, including profound and multiple disabilities; challenging behaviour; or associated mental health needs are the groups that could most benefit from self-directed support as a mechanism for taking control of their lives and breaking down *inappropriate patterns of services* (CSCI et al., 2009, page 13).

Perhaps the most fundamental impact of self-directed support for people with learning disabilities and the wider social care system is the emerging partnerships that are required if people are to really exercise choice, control and be active citizens within their communities. As we have seen, there is a change in the relationship between the person using social care services and professionals. There will also be new partnerships with family members and with people's circles of support and advocates. The social care market will evolve through changes to the commissioner–service provider relationship and the anticipated decrease in block contract arrangements with more people directly purchasing their own services.

Improved integration between services, particularly health and social care, will be critical if people are to effectively direct their own support. The active engagement of providers of 'universal services', such as housing, leisure and employment services, will also be crucial in ensuring people have increased choice, control and opportunities to make changes to their lives. There will also be increased emphasis on other structures, such as banks, insurance companies and accountancy services to respond more effectively to the needs of people who are directing their own support. In the event of such services and structures not adopting more flexible and person-centred responses to people with learning disabilities, the potential for people to truly direct their own support will remain extremely limited (Monk, 2006, page 68).

The notion of co-production will be at the centre of these changing relationships and will be supported by the drive to ensure that local Learning Disability Partnership Boards are delivering against the *Valuing People Now* agenda in their localities (DoH, 2009b, page vi). *The Valuing People Now* programme gives the local Learning Disability Partnership Board the responsibility to ensure that the personalisation agenda is embedded within local services and all developments that impact on the lives of people with learning disabilities and carers (DoH, 2009b, page 14). As a result, it is assumed that as the central means of co-production, local Learning Disability Partnership Boards are best placed to oversee the arrangements that support people with learning disabilities in local areas to benefit from self-directed support. Indeed, as part of the new Valuing People Now: Partnership Board Annual Self Assessment Reporting arrangements (commencing with annual reports produced from April 2010), local boards will be expected to report on the progress being made to develop, enhance and deliver self-directed support arrangements for people with learning disabilities in their local areas. This is likely to produce a more comprehensive future understanding of the extent to which people with learning disabilities are truly self-directing their own support arrangements across the country.

Conclusion

Self-directed support is a major theme across social policy. The national *Putting People First and Valuing People Now* agendas outline a challenging programme for ensuring that people with learning disabilities are given opportunities to direct their own support. There are clearly many powerful examples of how people with learning disabilities are directing their own support arrangements. Where this is happening effectively, there are powerful accounts of people experiencing real transformation in their lives and experiencing very outcomes from social care. As a result, people with learning disabilities are experiencing positive improved quality of life and increased choice, control, citizenship and social capital. The way people view themselves and how they are perceived by services will also change, with a shift in power from professionals to the individual themselves as 'co-producers' of care.

However, implementation of self-directed support is slow and variable across local authorities. There is evidence to suggest that people with learning disabilities and complex needs are not always given the full opportunity to self-direct their own support. Issues of risk, capacity, consent and responsibility are used as reasons for not offering self-directed support to people with learning disabilities. There are also concerns around the extent to which other people, such as professionals and informal carers, influence and control the person's choices.

It is clear that if self-directed support is to offer real choice, control and independence to people with learning disabilities, it should not be limited to social care only. People will come to expect greater flexibility and range of options to meet needs across all aspects of daily life, including health, housing and employment. Without this, it is difficult to see how self-directed support can truly make a difference to the lives of people with learning disabilities.

Self-directed support for people with learning disabilities is perceived in some quarters to be 'uncharted territory'. However, we must not fail to learn from the long history of effective person-centred planning with people with learning disabilities to support them to be involved in making decisions and changes to their lives. Learning must also be gained from the implementation of direct payments and the evaluation of the In Control pilots to ensure that people are given the best opportunities to take control of their lives through self-directed support. The challenges for implementation will be to scale up this learning so that wherever possible, self-directed support will be the standard approach for the majority rather than a minority of people. The scope and scale of change in culture, practice and the wider social forces cannot be underestimated.

The extent to which self-directed support is actually self-directed by people with learning disabilities should not be measured in terms of the number of people accessing individualised funding arrangements such as personal budgets or by how many person-centred support plans have been produced. Over time, the success of self-directed support should be evidenced by the accomplishment of increased community presence, co-production and active participation; people will be able to exercise their rights and responsibilities as citizens to expect fair access to high-quality services; and individuals will have a greater degree of independence, choice and control over their lives.

Chapter 7
Caring for older people: Informal care and carers

Professor Keith Brown

Introduction

...providing the services and support which people who are affected by problems of ageing, mental illness, mental handicap or physical or sensory disability need to be able to live as independently as possible in their own homes or in 'homely' settings in the community.

(DoH, 1989)

The reshaping of community care envisaged by the architects of the 1990 NHS and Community Care Act is predicted on a continuation – indeed an expansion – of what is increasingly referred to as the 'informal welfare sector' (a term apparently popularised by the Wolfenden and Barclay Reports 1978, 1982). Both the Griffiths Report, *Community Care: Agenda for Action,* and the 1989 White Paper, *Caring for People*, stress its centrality and the need for local authorities to:

arrange the delivery of packages of care building first on the available contribution of informal carers and neighbourhood support.

(DHSS, *Caring for People*, 1989)

The significance attached to the domestic and communal production of welfare in the current 'restructuring' of health and welfare services has, however, long been apparent. Indeed the blueprint for current proposals can be found in Norman Fowler's influential address to the Joint Social Services Conference in September 1984. Central to his concept of *a strategic and enabling role for social services departments* was the assertion that state provision of care should increasingly give way and tap into *a great reservoir of voluntary and private effort*. In the process he envisaged that tens of thousands would be able to *give back something to their own community by participating in social support* DHSS, 1984).

His promised Green Paper did not materialise, but the enhanced role of informal care remained a recurrent theme in policy statements and documents. As McCarthy argues, despite the protracted negotiations over agreeing the 'lead authority', a succession of reports throughout the 1980s were *setting in train new processes of socialisation that would alter expectations and perceptions about the levels and nature of care* (McCarthy, 1989, pages 43–5). Thus, to cite just a few examples – the 1981 Report, *Growing Older* (DHSS, 1981); (the 1986 Cumberledge Report (DHSS, 1986); the 1987 White Paper, *Promoting Better Health* (DoH, 1987); and SSI, *From Home Help to Care* and parts of the Project 2000 scheme, all prompted both the notion of the 'enabling' state and the 'front-line' role of informal 'helping networks'. A similar process of acclimatising both users and providers to a more pluralist economy of welfare can be traced in a stream of national and local initiatives – some of which pre-date the Fowler speech (e.g. 1976 Good Neighbour Scheme, 1981 Care in the Community, 1984 Helping the Community Care).

The significance attached to informal welfare is not confined to Britain. Similar attempts to utilise and encourage the 'community' to support dependent individuals were a central feature of social policy in many European countries in the 1980s.

In France for instance, the 1988 Braun Report (*Les Personnes Agées Dependantes*) priori-tised domiciliary support services for the elderly, and prompted both a more decentralised administrative system and greater co-ordination of statutory and independent health and welfare system providers and improved liaison with carers. (As in Belgium, families in France are legally responsible for the maintenance of their elderly relatives, and tax allow-ances reinforce this principle.) De-institutionalisation and an emphasis on 'home' care for other 'dependant' groups is a central feature of current social policy planning debates in other EEC states too, notably Italy, Belgium and Germany. In the US, recent attempts to residualise state welfare incorporated a wide-ranging campaign to highlight the crucial role of informal state welfare and self-provisioning (Gilbert, 1983; David, 1986; Mangen, 1985; Hill, 1991; Kraan et al., 1990; Munday, 1989).

In Sweden recent policy reviews have entailed paid leave for carers and the payment of carers. In Britain at a political level, and, indeed, in many of the responses to the 1990 Act, the value and potential of the informal sector remain unquestioned. Some commentators, however, have expressed considerable doubts about the assumed caring capacity of the 'community'. Whether such concerns are justified depends partly on one's assessment of research findings on the 'demand' for care, the current patterning of informal care and its growth potential. It also depends on one's concept of 'community care'. This chapter aims to facilitate discussion of these key issues through a review both of empirical research and sociological discourse on 'community' in contemporary Britain. (Time constraints prevent a similar exploration of recent American and European studies.) It is hoped the concerns raised will facilitate consideration of the principles and practice of 'case management' and 'care packaging'.

Perspectives on 'community care' and 'informal care'

A cursory scan of the literature reveals considerable confusion and ambiguity in both nomenclature and use of the concept of 'informal care'. Indeed it is frequently used inter-changeably with 'community care'. As numerous commentators have observed, this, in turn, is a concept with infinitely *flexible meanings* (Pascal, 1986, page 86). Writing in the 1960s, Titmuss highlighted both the normative and prescriptive elements of such an emotive term, seeing community care as characteristic of attempts *to employ idealistic terms to describe certain branches of public policy* entailing the danger that *in the public mind the aspirations of reformers are transmuted by touch of phrase into hardened reality*. (Titmuss, 1968, page 104).

Indeed reviewing the manifold definitional problems involved and the extent to which prescription merges with description, one is tempted to agree with those who argue that the term *means little in itself* and should be abandoned – particularly in view of the *trail of confusion* created (Smith, 1989, page 626).

Within sociology too the concept of 'community' is often presented as *one of the most elusive and vague ... now largely without specific meaning* (Abercrombie, 1994). Nevertheless it is possible to discern the major usages:

- it is used to refer to a locality/given geographical area;

- it is used to describe a local social system/set of social relationships which centre on a particular locality;

- it is employed to denote a type of relationship which is characterised by a strong sense of shared identity (based on common experiences/interests but not necessarily common residence).

The relevance of the first two usages to advance urban industrial societies has long been debated by sociologists, and a number have suggested that it is the third usage which most conforms to individual experiences in contemporary society, while the first two are characteristic only of certain neighbourhoods and certain stages in the life cycle.

Attempts to clarify the concepts of 'community' and 'community care' in policy terms have tended to concur in a distinction between the usages:

- 'Care in the community' (usually presented as the antithesis of institutional care);

- 'Care by the community'.

There is a general consensus that the policy of community care originated in the post-war reaction to institutional forms of care. This was evidenced in the 1940s in child care and from the 1950s in the treatment of the mentally ill, the elderly and the disabled. The twin pressures of cost-efficiency and concern over the damaging effects of 'total institutions' (along with, in the case of the mentally ill, new drug treatments) led to a succession of measures designed to reduce institutional provision. With the 1959 Mental Health Act and more especially the 1962 Hospital Health Plan and the associated Health and Welfare Report of 1963, the contraction of traditional institutional care was 'connected' with residential units and non-residential services provided by local authorities. (Walker, 1982, in Smith, 1989; Jones, 1989, provide helpful surveys of these developments; a revisionist account, stressing pressures in the 1950s Ministry of Health to avoid the heavy costs of expanding and refurbishing inherited institutions, is provided by Goodwin, (1989/1990); 'feminist' accounts by Finch, in Ungerson (1990); and Langan (1990), develop a three-phase chronological account.)

More recently, the 2007 Mental Health Act saw the introduction of supervised community treatment (SCT), allowing a number of people to live in the community, subject to certain conditions. The White Paper, Our Health, Our care, Our Say (DoH, 2006a), set out its vision for more people being supported in their homes, having more choice and being able to remain active and independent in their own homes. Individual budgets are at the heart of government policy to enable this to happen.

As a plethora of studies have shown however, the first version of community care *existed largely at the level of political rhetoric. It was never clearly and consistently defined, and the political will in the form of policy-making and planning machinery, and especially resource allocation and re-allocation were never mobilised* (Walker, in McCarthy, 1989, page 205). Despite repeated exhortations to local and health authorities to develop community-based substitutes for institutional care, and the introduction of joint planning and funding in the late 1970s (belatedly including the voluntary sector), by the mid-1980s it was clear that *community care was grounded; more precisely it had never taken off* (Barritt, 1990, page 9).

The manifest failure of the policy can be variously accounted for, with professional rivalry figuring high alongside political mismanagement in many accounts. (Indeed 'professional networks' may prove as crucial to case management in practice as the mobilisation of informal carers.) One factor which attracted increasing attention in the late 1970s, however, was the concept of community care implicit in the early measures. From the 1950s it appears that community care was perceived in terms of care provided by statutory agencies and their professional and ancillary personnel, primarily on a domiciliary basis, but also through 'homely' residential units, located in the 'community'. The latter continued to dominate both health and social service budgets and was included in DHSS programming from the 1970s. Nevertheless, the concept of 'care in the community' conceived as non/less institutionalised provision, collectively funded, and delivered by public agencies dominated official pronouncements.

With the changed economic and ideological climate from the late 1970s, it appears that 'community care' has been re-conceptualised as 'care by the community':

> *Whatever level of public expenditure proves practicable, and however it is distributed, the primary sources of support and care are informal and voluntary ... It is the role of public authorities to sustain and where necessary to develop – but never to displace – such support and care. Care IN the community must increasingly mean care BY the community.*

> (DHSS, *Growing Older*, 1981, page 3).

A reading of the official documents and pronouncements suggests this is viewed as the provision of welfare and healthcare by relatives, neighbours, friends and other personal contacts. In one of the few early studies of such 'welfaring', Abrams provided what is probably still the most used definition:

> *provision of help, support and protection by lay members of societies acting in everyday domestic and occupational settings.*

> (Abrams, 1977, page 125)

In this sense 'community care' becomes transposed into 'informal care' and it is this trans-posed version that appears to be uppermost in current policy-making (supplemented by voluntary and private-market provision, either individually organised or 'packaged' by revamped local authorities).

This redefinition of community care can be seen simply as an acknowledgement of the fail-ure of the earlier concept and a recognition of the extent to which the 'care gap' created by hospital closures and the underdevelopment of local authority services for both those 'decanted' and 'non-admissions' had apparently been filled by alternative care. As with the earlier 'anti-institutionalism' it can also be read as an attempt to ensure more 'natural' support for dependent groups. But it is also possible however, to interpret this redefinition of community care as intrinsic to *a new era of welfare that owes as much to the mores and values of the market as it does to social service and care* (McCarthy,1989, page 9).

In more recent years we have seen the introduction of direct payments and individualised budgets (DoH, 2005b). Individualised budgets aim to bring together resources from differ-ent funding streams to allow for more choice and flexibility, thus enabling people to have more control over their lives and the care they receive.

Patterns of caring: Family-based care

However one perceives the 'mixed economy of welfare' envisaged by the 1990 Act, its implementation is conditional on the continued – and expanding – support of the infor-mal sector. Yet despite an upsurge in research in the last decade, an understanding of the characteristics and functioning of the helping networks available to dependent individuals in non-residential care is still uneven.

Ideally, any assessment should encompass not only types of relationship (family/other, etc.), the number, range, frequency and duration of contacts between the 'cared for' and 'carer(s)', the tasks undertaken and services provided, but also the meanings attached to the relationship by the different participants. By its very nature however, much of the help provided is currently unrecorded and also extremely difficult to both access and quantify, let alone assess. Nevertheless, the redirection of policy spawned a mass of research, both 'micro' and 'macro'. In particular, detailed analyses of the 1985 General Household Survey and the OPCS & Disablement Survey appeared, giving new insight into both the numbers and characteristics of various 'dependent' groups and those who identified themselves as 'carers' (i.e. individuals who *look after or give special help to or provide some regular serv-ice or help for any sick, handicapped person, adult or child*). Many of the key findings have been usefully collated by Parker (1985, 1990). Further summaries are provided by Evandrou (1990); Twigg, (1989); and Perring (1989).

Evandrou's survey leads her to estimate that 14 per cent of those over 16, i.e. one in seven adults or 6 million people, were caring for a sick, elderly or handicapped person. Parker endorses the 6 million figure for Great Britain, but argues that only 3.7 million should be seen as 'helping' adults disabled enough to be included in the OPCS survey, with 1.3 mil-lion as 'main carers' (as in her 1985 estimate). Indeed, there is now considerable debate over both the numbers and characteristics of 'carers' (Redding, 1991).

Carers UK state that 3 in 5 will be informal carers sometime in their lives, providing support valued at £87 billion.

Most research has focused on 'family' care rather than that of friends or neighbours. Before reviewing the main findings, however, it is crucial to recognise that the term 'family', like 'community', is open to different interpretations. Conventionally, sociologists have long distinguished between the 'nuclear' and 'extended' family. Traditionally, the former was perceived in terms of a married couple plus their offspring, the unspoken assumption being that the couple comprised a male breadwinner and a female 'homemaker'.

It is contestable whether this family form was ever the 'norm', and current research clearly demonstrates that the 'cereal packet' image is now only one of a diversity of family structures in contemporary society. It appears, however, that much social legislation is still permeated by traditionalist concepts of both the nuclear family and its links with extended kin – and such thinking seems to underpin the 'care by the community' programme. The compatibility between this and current/projected 'family' trends will be raised later. For now, recognition of this 'pluralism' is the essential backcloth to any research review. Indeed some sociologists prefer to refer to 'household' rather than 'family' to explicate the patterning of 'care'.

Drawing on the newly available studies it is possible to distinguish a number of common themes in family care. First, a substantial body of research, stretching back to the 1950s, has attempted to demythologise the frequently repeated assertion that state welfare has undermined family care for dependants. Hadley and Hatch encapsulated the general finding:

> *Most of the care that is provided for dependent people living in their own homes comes not from the state, nor from voluntary organisations, nor from commercial sources, but from family, friends and neighbours.*

> (Hadley and Hatch, 1981, page 87)

This general conclusion was endorsed by a stream of 'family studies' in the 1980s. Often a by-product of (feminist-inspired) concern at the differential employment patterns of men and women, such studies have documented the care provided in or through the family for a range of client groups. Moreover, recent historical research suggests that the contemporary family is providing more support than in the past (Wall, 1990).

Secondly, studies of different dependent groups, while emphasising differential needs, have also identified a number of common strands in the patterning of 'family' resourced care.

Household/non-household based care
Evandrou's data suggest 1.7m adults care for a 'co-resident' (4 per cent of all adults); 4.25 million for someone outside their household (10 per cent of all adults).

As highly dependent on one 'primary carer'
Though this was implicit in earlier research and emphasised by studies of 'single' carers, its prevalence within 'families' is only now being documented. It appears that once an individual is perceived as the 'carer', support from other relatives (and friends) tends to disappear. The processes whereby such 'invisible' carers 'emerge' has been explored by

Ungerson (1987), who stresses the role of co/proximate residence, age, other commitments and especially gender in this process. Evandrou suggests females are more likely to be 'sole' carers; males 'peripheral' carers, though 'joint' caring is less 'skewed'. The first are most likely to be caring for spouses; peripheral carers for other relatives/friends, and joint carers for a parent-in-law. Sole carers are likely to be the most 'disadvantaged' in natural terms and also the most 'stressed'.

The gendered nature of care

Initial research into various client groups in the 1980s suggested that *the majority of carers are women* and *the majority of women will at some time in their lives be carers* (EOC, 1982, page iii). This division of labour appeared to operate along several dimensions, in terms of:

- the numbers of female/male carers;
- the age at which caring starts/length of the caring 'career';
- the source of the relationship (males tend to care for spouses; females for other relatives too);
- the type of tasks and services provided;
- the amount and length of time spent caring;
- support from other family members/ contacts;
- help from statutory/other sources.

The general conclusion of the early studies is well summarised in the notion of 'the double equation': *in practice, community care equals care by family, and in practice care by the family equals care by women* (Finch and Groves, 1980, page 494). It appeared to run counter to equal-opportunities legislation.

A number of studies explored the differential pressures underpinning this division of labour and related taboos surrounding 'cross-sex caring'. While some have focused on the complexities of family history and interpersonal relationships in determining 'caring', most are framed in terms of different feminist analyses (Dalley, 1988; Lewis and Meredith, 1988).

Male carers

In contrast, some later studies, notably those of Arber and Gilbert (1989), suggest men make a larger contribution than had been recognised and – in the case of the infirm elderly – it is household type (single/couple/presence of unmarried younger members) rather than gender which determines external support. Evandrou too argues that *men are far more involved in providing informal care than previously thought* (1990, page 29). Indeed, 2.5 million of the 6 million carers in her study were male. Parker's research review, however, leads her to conclude that, *in the population at large, women provide the bulk of care* and that there has been little shift in the division of care (1990, page 56). The relative role of the 'new male' in this – as other areas of 'family' life – is likely to remain controversial. What is clear, however, is that the majority of male carers are caring for spouses

– care of others is still primarily, in practice, a female task. It may also be that the form of survey/questioning used in some studies leads to higher male 'self-reporting', with women taking care work more 'for granted'.

The costs of care

As has been frequently noted, the impulse to both versions of 'community care' has been primarily cost-driven. From the outset, 'care in the community' was seen as a cheaper as well as a more therapeutic and personalised alternative to institutionalisation. Yet, as the Short Committee trenchantly suggested, *the proposition that community care could be cost-neutral is untenable* and if fully implemented 'care in the community' could prove more expensive than a continuation of residential provision (Social Services Committee, 1985, page ixv).

It is also clear from official sources that 'care by the community' is seen as ensuring 'affordable' cost effective care. But again, most studies testify an implicit 'creative accountancy' which fails to quantify the hidden costs of informal care. For the prime carer, these 'costs' are now well established if unmitigated.

- The cost in terms of the drain on carers' physical health.

- The impact on carers' mental health.

- The stress placed on marital and other family relationships.

- The loss of employment and education opportunities, both short and long term and the associated life time earnings.

- The extra financial costs entailed in servicing the varied special needs of 'cared for' individuals.

- The loss of social contacts and 'non-obligated time'.

- The added pressure of managing direct payments and individualised budgets and finding one's own care.

Evandrou suggests that carers as a group are likely to experience relative impoverishment, but that sole carers have a higher probability of low income, with female sole carers being particularly disadvantaged. Carers with co-resident dependants were more likely to experience poverty than those caring for someone outside the home (Evandrou, 1990, page 1). As feminists such as Land and Graham have frequently argued, caring, particularly when undertaken by women, sustains not one but two forms of dependency. Ironically, as Glendinning's recent research shows, the 'carer' can become financially dependent on the 'cared for' – and face further impoverishment on the latter's decease or admission to permanent care (see e.g. Land 1989; Glendinning and Baldwin, 1988; Glendinning, 1990).

The quality of 'family' care

Most research tended to focus on the carer's perspectives, though this 'imbalance' has been rectified, notably by Quareshi and Walker (1989). What emerges from this, as in other studies, is the highly variable nature of both the rewards and the strains inherent in 'caring'. By its very nature, any assessment of the quality of such care, grounded as it is in pre-existing relationships and separate from the 'performance indicators' currently being developed for formal services, is obviously highly subjective. One salient conclusion, neglected in much of the debate about 'community care', but familiar to those involved in child care is that family care can be both *the best and the worst form of care* (Quareshi and Walker, page 240). (It is perhaps worth noting that two 'elder abuse' journals are already being published in the USA.) It is also worth noting that several recent studies suggest many of the 'cared for' prefer some degree of reciprocity in relation to their 'carers'. Indeed the few 'user'-based investigations suggest that many of those diagnosed as 'mentally ill' have more positive perceptions of institutional care than that provided in/by 'the community' (Chapman et al., 1991).

Caring for different forms of dependency

Within these overall general patterns, however, it is crucial to recognise that expectations and practices about who should care and where, vary with the type and age of the dependent. Disabled children are seen as primarily a parental (in practice maternal) responsibility. However, attitudes towards the care of adults diverge according to whether the disability/illness develops after a 'normal' life in 'old age', or whether it was manifest in childhood. While the role of the 'prime carer' within the 'family' is now well recognised in each 'area', what is not clear is the possible variability of other relatives' support according to the nature of the dependency.

'Neighbouring' and 'helping networks'

In contrast to the morass of research into family-centred care, the notion of a surrounding layer of informal carers has, with a few notable exceptions, remained until very recently, largely untested. The indirect evidence supplied by the numerous family studies, however, suggests that the contribution of non-relatives is generally minimal and highly restricted both in terms of the quantity and quality of support offered. General studies of friendship patterns and local social structures (not necessarily emanating from concern with social policy) provide insights into the constraints on this wider source of informal care.

For instance, Allen, like many others, emphasises two distinctive characteristics of friendship: friends (unlike kin and neighbours) are chosen, and the relationship hinges on reciprocity. One's friends must bring *equivalent financial and emotional resources to the relationship* and while 'caring about' may be a facet of the relationship, 'caring for' is not an inherent component (Allen, 1985, page 137). In his more recent, extended attempt to initiate a sociology of friendship (including class/gender/ethnic/life cycle differences) he reiterates the 'short-termism' of many friendships, the many circumstantial constraints which prevent friends 'caring' for either a 'dependent' individual or a 'carer', and above all the intrinsically reciprocal exchange base of contemporary friendship patterns, the symmetry of which is disrupted by *a continuing need for unilateral care* (Allen, 1990, page 113).

Neighbours may become friends, but this is usually based on some form of reciprocity too, involving (alongside 'socialising') restricted exchanges of such services as looking after the property or keys during one's absence, offering lifts or babysitting and 'borrowing and lending' of various kinds. The extent of such 'neighbouring' emerges from a wealth of community studies. As one of the most indefatigable investigators into local networks, Wilmott, suggests such 'support' is not easily translated into 'caring'. This emerges clearly from his useful classification of different forms of informal care into:

- personal care/tending /human maintenance;

- domestic care;

- auxiliary care;

- social support;

- surveillance.

Given the reciprocity inherent in 'neighbouring' it appears that the restricted and short-term categories (social support) and (surveillance) involving low emotional investment and personal commitment are those most likely to be resourced by neighbours. Even here, however, such help is 'patchy' (Wilmott, 1986; Sharkey, 1989; Wenger, 1990).

Quareshi and Walker's Sheffield study (1989) leads to the same conclusion, as does Finch's (1989). Such findings were anticipated by Abrams' pioneering studies. These led him to reject 'romanticised notions' of spontaneous altruism in favour of the notion that care-giving *is a self interested activity*. Non-kin (and even family) care in contemporary society was *typically volatile, spasmodic and unreliable* and *invariably tied to perceptions of long or short term reciprocal advantage* (Abrams, 1977, pages 125–132). A later edition of his – and others' – research into 'good neighbourhood' schemes support his earlier findings, highlighting the emergence of 'new neighbourhoodism' consequent on post-war housing developments. Most people, he argued, live in new neighbourhoods and their relationships are not only highly privatised but instrumental – participation in locally based mutual aid being contingent on a calculation of likely costs/benefits. The only features of traditional neighbourliness to have survived, he concluded, were 'mothers and gossip'. In such circumstances, attempts to revive/draw on local social networks appeared 'misguided' (Bulmer, 1987). It could be argued that even in the 'classic slum' setting or small hamlet where shared residence and experiences appear to have fostered neighbourly interdependence, recent research provides *little evidence to support the idea that non-kin played a major part in caring, except in times of crisis* (Allen, 1990). More significant now, however, is the common concern in many studies that contemporary lifestyles and residential patterns disable even limited 'neighbouring'.

The role of personal social services

From the Barclay Report on, there has been pressure to 'interweave' informal and statutory care, but most research documents a mismatch between the latter and the essentially female-based pattern of informal care (contributing to attempts at improved planning and delivery). Writing in 1985, Parker concluded that *available services are likely to have little overall effect for informal carers*. Firstly, few dependent people who have carers appear to receive services, and when they do, such services are crisis-oriented rather than part of long-term support. Secondly, the criteria by which services are allocated are often irrational (not allocated in relation to need) and discriminatory (not provided where female carers are available) (Parker, 1985, page 88). Both the Short Report (1985) and the Audit Commission (1986) reached similar conclusions, and the former also drew attention to the neglect of the particular needs of ethnic minority carers and their dependants. Reviewing conventional health and welfare provision in 1990, Parker still found they *have little overall effect for informal carers*, repeating the same points made in 1985 (1990, page 125). Her findings have been endorsed by Twigg et al. (1990), and Barritt's (1990) Innovations in Community Care Survey. Despite initiatives such as carers' forums, carers' handbooks, family hospitality and other 'sit-in' schemes, genuine support for carers was far from the norm.

Under-resourcing and interprofessional rivalry are held partly responsible for this mismatch. But a number of studies suggest it is also a reflection of 'received ideas' among health and social workers about both 'dependency' and informal caring, the latter being conceived primarily as a female responsibility (Rojek, 1988; Quareshi and Walker, 1989; Dalley, 1988). A further factor appears to be the prevalence of 'received ideas' on the family patterns of different ethnic groups in Britain (Atkin, 1991).

Twigg has developed a provisional classification of the 'frames of reference' used by health and especially social workers in dealing with carers. As she emphasises, care is usually structured around the client with concern for the carer being a more 'instrumental' by-product of this. In her ideal type construction, a care workers' model of the carer can take three possible forms. These are:

- carers as resources (though undirectable and uncommandable);

- carers as co-workers;

- carers as co-clients.

All three, however, entail a common tension generated by a concept of 'success' which takes *passage into residential care as a crucial service indicator* and thus, from a carer's perspective can appear to *reward failure* (Twigg, 1989, pages 62–3; also in Jamieson and Illsley, 1991). Recent studies of the 'carer-service provider interface' suggest a further dimension, that of the carer as 'co-claimant'/'advocate'. Assumption of this role, however, is contingent on the carers' knowledge-base and the promotional/intervention strategies of SSDs. Carers' potential as a 'pressure group' however, may well be restricted by factors similar to those inhibiting 'industrial action' among low-waged female workers. (Sinclair, et al., and Hunter and Macpherson, in Jamieson and Illsley, 1991).

Social protection and informal care

This has been a much-neglected aspect of informal care. But a growing number of studies have explored the correspondence/lack of correspondence between the financial costs and dependency/caring and the support systems available. The potential for 'carers' to become financially dependent on the 'cared for' and the life-cycle/pension entitlements implications for women carers taking 'career breaks'/part-time employment have already been raised (see too Glendinning, 1990; Finnister, 1991). Many studies echo Johnson's finding that the current emphasis on community and family care *might be more acceptable if statutory financial support for families were more generous* and the needs of both carers/cared for were recognised rather than undermined by recent social security measures (M. Johnson, 1990, page 148). Indeed it is frequently presented as not only more 'natural' and less rigid than 'bureaucratic/professional' public care systems, but as preserving the 'independence' of the individual concerned. It is perhaps worth considering whether family care necessarily reduces 'dependence'.

The caring capacity of the community

Whatever the specifics of research into the parameters of informal care, however, in Britain its significance appears unquestioned. The assumption central to current policy that it provides an underused and expandable reservoir of care capable of meeting the increase in 'dependency' projected by both the 'ageing' of Britain and the increased incidence/survival of other 'dependants', is also questionable. Johnson captures this new concern, suggesting that *we should be asking not whether the family can provide more care in the future but whether it will even be able to maintain its current level of provision*. (N. Johnson, 1990, page 127). Moreover:

> The wholesale transfer of responsibility from the state to informal carers, which some New Right theorist's advocate, is likely to lead to falling standards of care and intolerable pressures on families. There are limits to the extra work which families can absorb, and those limits may already have been reached. The informal sector is in no position to compensate for a reduction in the state's role. Indeed, if informal care is to continue at its present level, state support of the family will have to be increased.

(M. Johnson, 1990, page 151)

Such concerns are not confined to Britain – a European study of family patterns concluded *the traditional sources of family care for all vulnerable members can no longer be taken for granted, implying a growing bill for ... governments* (Robbins, 1990, page 103).

Feminist writers in particular have highlighted the extent to which shifts in population age structures, employment patterns and family relationships (including rising divorce rates) indicate possible problems in sustaining informal care work in the future. Other research into kinship networks raises similar concerns about the changing pattern of such relationships. Wilmott, for instance, suggests there are *three broad kinship arrangements* in contemporary Britain: *the local extended family* (characteristic of one in eight of the adult population), *the dispersed extended family* (characteristic of half the adult population) and *the attenuated extended family* (Wilmott, 1987).

Reviewing studies of the 'informal sector', Allen concludes *any attempt to influence networks of neighbours, friends, and kin so as to encourage greater support and varying for members in need would not be so much an extension of 'natural' networks as a wholly artificial manipulation of them* (Allen,1991, page 121). Moreover, as Foster argues, *there is very little reason to suppose that non-compulsory altruism will break out* among 'non carers' (Foster, 1991).

In response to such concerns, and as part of the wider effort to create 'non-sexist' welfare policies and practices, some were advocating greater use of residential and/or paid domiciliary care. This however, is conceived in 'non-traditional' gender-neutral terms and also emphasises customised consumerist practices (Finch, 1984; Dalley, 1988; Foster, 1991).

Conclusion

The feasibility and modes of improving the position of carers, while both 'weakening sexual divisions in caring', and 'maximising opportunities for independence for older people or those with disabilities', is highly controversial, and a range of possible measures are being canvassed, including new financial schemes for both 'carers'/'cared for' (see e.g. Baldwin and Twigg, 1991; Baldock and Ungerson, (1991); Glennerster et al., 1990; and – from a different perspective – Ramon, 1991, which emphasises the need to incorporate a multidimensional concept of 'normalisation', into both policy and practice in the 'new' community care regime). Most, however, assume a state- rather than a market-based commercially driven response, emphasising the need for more innovative delivery systems, not the abandonment of public provision *in favour of some idealised and unrealistic notion of 'family care'* (Jamieson and Illsley, 1991, page 19).

One's response depends on how one interprets current demographic and social trends, and on one's assessment of some of the alternative concepts and models of care that are currently being canvassed. However, it is clear that in the twenty-first century, the pressure on the state to provide care for vulnerable adults is rapidly growing as the capacity of the informal carers is under greater pressure. Changes in family structure, the need for potential informal carers to work full time to pay for mortgages and associated housing costs and also to ensure they have sufficient pension provision for the future, coupled with a society which appears to be moving more towards a moral position that reduces the perception of a moral duty/responsibility to care for one's relatives, all put further pressure on the state as the potential pool of informal carers contracts. Added to this is the new coalition government's recognition of the need to reform the system of social care, including a greater roll-out of personal budgets, in the context of the current economic crisis and the government's plan to cut grants to English councils by £1.2 billion in 2010–11.

Chapter 8

Promoting inclusiveness: Developing empowering practice with minority groups of older people

Dr Lee-Ann Fenge

Introduction

Recognising the diversity of experience within the British ageing population has been supported by policy which promotes person-centred and anti-ageist practice (DoH, 2001b; Office of the Deputy Prime Minister, 2006). However, older lesbians and gay men have traditionally received little interest from service providers and hetero-normative assumptions have dominated both theory and practice concerning old age (Cronin, 2006). It is therefore important for practitioners to acknowledge that older people do not represent a homogenous group, and that there is great diversity of experience not only within the ageing population, but also within lesbian and gay experiences of ageing (Musingarimi, 2008).

Background

Historically, social work departments have structured their work with older people on the basis of ageist assumptions, oversimplifying their needs as being routine, and using largely unqualified staff to assess the needs of older service users (Lymbery, 2005). A move towards increased personalisation and self-assessment (DoH, 2005b) goes some way to redress this imbalance, and encourages the older person to be central within the assessment of their needs. A key element within developing social work practice with older lesbians and gay men is their liberation from dominant knowledge and power practices, and this requires the development of new knowledge from research to improve practitioners' understanding of the needs of this diverse group. This is particularly important for 'minority' groups of older people who have traditionally been invisible from mainstream service provision. Postmodernism has evolved a worldview that acknowledges there is no one way of knowing, no one way of being, and no one way of experiencing reality (Warburton, 1994). It is therefore important to open up social work's professional knowledge base to critical scrutiny (Pease, 2002), and to embrace knowledge that evolves from *inside a culture* (Swantz, 1996, page 124), rather than being purely defined by 'outside' professional knowledge and language. This supports the development of research methods which engage with older lesbians and gay men to enable them to steer the research and growing evidence base in this area of practice.

The impact of ageism

Ageism represents a key feature of the discrimination and oppression that all older people experience, and therefore the fundamental basis of practice with older people must be anti-ageist. Central to this is recognising that older people as a group are subject to discrimination and oppression on both macro and micro levels within society (Thompson, 1998b). The National Service Framework for Older People (DoH, 2001b) in Britain highlighted the need to tackle ageist practice within health and social care, and counteract the negativity associated with ageing at personal, cultural and structural levels within society.

A society that reflects negative images about ageing and older people will have a negative impact on those who are older and drives a wedge between the young and old. The image of frailty and vulnerability in old age is powerful (Herring and Thom, 1997), and influences how both the public and practitioners view older people. Practitioners can underestimate the impact of ageism on older people, and this can increase the dehumanisation that many older people experience (Milner and O'Byrne, 1998). As a result, older people can be seen as non-persons, their needs and views being overlooked by professionals who see themselves as expert in defining their needs and developing service provision.

Another key feature of ageism is that it categorises older people as a homogenous group (Thompson and Thompson, 2001) and diversity of experience and difference is lost in stereotypical assumptions about ageing and decline. Therefore some older people may face further discrimination and oppression on the basis of their gender, sexuality, ethnicity or disability.

A number of research studies have uncovered a range of factors which influence the experience of ageing for older lesbians and gay men. The relationships that older gay men and lesbians have are often limited by economic, social and cultural resources (Heaphy, 2009). The importance of 'acceptance' as a guiding principle within practice has been highlighted, and alongside this is the need for lesbian and gay-friendly services including bereavement counselling, buddying schemes, gay-friendly advocacy, home support and gay-specific information in public areas (Gay and Grey in Dorset, 2006, page 71).

Sexuality

Oppression is a key feature in the lives of older lesbian women and gay men. Oppression is experienced not only through ageism but may also be experienced through heterosexism (Berkman and Zinberg, 1997), which permeates our culture and social institutions, and through homophobia (Hudson and Ricketts, 1980).

As Musingarimi (2008) suggests, there exists great diversity of experience with the ageing experiences of older lesbians and gay men. Fear of discrimination and oppression may influence whether or not an individual decides to 'come out' within their local community (Edwards, 2005; Musingarimi, 2008). Some older individuals have lived with the fear that exposure would devastate their lives and many have felt isolated and ashamed of their feelings (Bohan, 1996). As homosexuality was illegal in Britain until 1963 and a mental disorder until 1973, many will have endured medical interventions (D'Augelli et al., 2001) or been prosecuted. This is likely to have resulted in feelings of stigma and shame, which has gone on to shape their lives (Brotman et al., 2003). In order to live in safety many gay men acquired a wife and had discreet sexual relations with men. For women, society deemed living with female roommates as acceptable and thus they often passed as this and nothing more (Quam, 1993).

The effects of living a concealed life, however, can be seen as having a lasting detriment, as some individuals continue to feel abnormal. After concealing a large part of themselves for the majority of their lives, many are still coming to terms with the effects of homophobia, including low self-esteem, a fear of disclosing their sexuality and a loss of relationships with family and friends (Hays et al., 1997). As a result they may experience weaker levels of social embeddedness, which might be linked to increased experiences of loneliness and isolation (Fokkema and Kuyper, 2009). It may also prevent them from approaching social services and other agencies when in need (Jacobs et al., 1999).

Alternatively, some lesbians and gay men are now ageing as a generation who have lived most of their lives as 'out' lesbians or gay men (Beeler et al., 1999) and may have much more positive experiences in later life. 'Coming out' can be seen as a process of developing awareness and acknowledgement of homosexual thoughts and feelings, and results in public awareness of one's identity (Davies, 1996). One of the predominant factors determining how older lesbians and gay men adjust to ageing is how they feel about their sexuality. D'Augelli et al. (2001) found that individuals with a positive view towards their sexuality had better mental health, a finding echoed by Deacon et al. (1995), who reported that high life satisfaction and low self-criticism was related to feeling positive about being gay. Research has shown that older lesbians and gay men who cope less well with ageing are commonly those with an internalised homophobia, developed through keeping their sexuality a secret. Because of this secrecy, many individuals felt guilty and ashamed, which when internalised and not resolved, inevitably leads to low self-esteem, greater social isolation (Jacobs et al., 1999) and poor mental health (D'Augelli et al., 2001).

For practitioners, it is important to be aware of the social construction of sexuality and the impact that religion, social and political beliefs and values have on the way older lesbian women and gay men are perceived by society. For example, managing stigma and exposure to discrimination over long periods of time has also been shown to result in higher risks of depression and suicide, addictions and substance abuse (Brotman et al., 2003). However, other research has suggested that 80 per cent of women and 62 per cent of men felt that their sexuality had enriched their lives (Heaphy et al., 2003). The experience of stigma is not just an individual experience, but can be seen as a tool of social inequality which reinforces the social exclusion of certain groups within society, and therefore power inequality is an important part of this experience (Parker and Aggleton, 2003).

The impact of heterosexism is that service providers have traditionally tailored their services to meet the needs of the heterosexual population (Jacobs et al., 1999). Although older lesbian women and gay men have the same needs as heterosexual older people, they will have experienced ageing differently. Therefore they require health and social care services that respond to their own particular needs. This includes the importance of spending as much time with and being supported by fellow gay men and lesbian women (Langley, 1997; Beeler et al., 1999) and the need for acceptance (Gay and Grey in Dorset, 2006).

Social work practitioners therefore need to develop their awareness of the invisibility and oppression experienced by older lesbians and gay men, and also develop sensitivity to allow them to voice their experiences and share their situated knowledge in order to develop practice and service provision. Recognition of and valuing difference is central to this process.

Empowerment

Empowerment, although *a contested concept* (Means and Smith, 1998, page 70), has been seen to be *the keystone of social work* (Lee, 2000, page 34). There arc a number of radical perspectives on empowerment, including those which talk of empowerment in terms of *challenging and combating oppression* (Ward and Mullender, 1991, page 22) and those which equate it with being able to exercise power or take control of oneself (Braye and Preston-Shoot, 1995, page 48). This perhaps can be broadly seen to link into notions of 'citizenship' and 'rights'. One way of viewing citizenship is in terms of participation, and as such participation *can be seen as representing an expression of human agency* (Lister, 1998, page 27). This could be seen in terms of political activity or voting, but also through less formal means such as participation in local community activities, family life, or social work assessment processes.

The inability to 'participate', or restrictions placed on participation, are central to this discussion. For many older people, 'participation' may be prevented by ageist assumptions about the value of older people within society and the negative connotations attached to ageing within a Western culture, and older gay men and lesbian women may be excluded further by discrimination and oppression related to gender or sexuality.

Researchers have identified the 'invisibility' of older gay men and lesbians, both within and outside the gay and lesbian community (Wahler and Gabbay, 1999; Fullmer et al., 1999). Some suggest that like the older population in general, older gay and lesbians are often socially isolated, and that they find themselves 'disengaged' from the lesbian and gay community (Jacobs et al., 1999). The stereotypical image of the ageing gay man includes someone who is 'excluded' from a 'youthist' gay culture, lonely, sexless and depressed (Wahler and Gabbay, 1999). Similar negative stereotypes exist for older lesbians, including being lonely, asexual and unattractive (Berger, 1982; Fullmer et al., 1999) Within the homosexual community, these negative stereotypes may 'set' older people apart from the younger members of the community and add to their 'invisibility'. The idealisation of youth which may be common within the gay community may drive a wedge between young and old and may displace older gay men from the social spaces previously open to them within the gay community (Murray and Adam, 2001). A focus on 'citizenship' can therefore help to promote emancipatory forms of social work practice which highlight rights to participation and inclusion.

Emancipatory approaches to social work practice and research focus on social change at both an individual and structural level. Anti-oppressive practice requires 'power sharing', and a move away from approaches which focus on the expertise of the practitioner to those which focus on the participation and expertise of the service user. Approaches to research which adopt participatory methodologies which engage with older people as experts and co-researchers have been undertaken in recent years (Fenge, 2010; Ward et al., 2008). Such approaches enable the voices of a previously hidden group to be heard and can enable social work to engage in partnership to generate new knowledge to help transform society (Barbera, 2008).

Social work practice

A move towards increased personalisation and personal narrative within the assessment process is aimed at ensuring a more person-centred approach to assessment, while encouraging professionals to work much more closely with service users. This approach values person-centred care and independence, and the older person's views and wishes should be central to this assessment process. Good practice is suggested by adopting a user narrative approach in the form of a biography in the older person's own words. The idea of a 'critical dialogue' (Freire, 1972) can be seen as important within this process as it centres upon the notion of sharing and acknowledgment. This can be seen as an important principle both within practice and research with older gay men and lesbian women as it values diversity of experience and meaning (Pollner and Rosenfield, 2000).

This may enable older lesbian and gay men to 'co-author' their assessments using language they choose to represent themselves. This may include whether or not to 'come out' to the assessor. This narrative approach is supported by research by Richards (2000), which supports the focus on user perspective. She suggests that it *will tend to reduce the power imbalance between elders and practitioners, as practitioners strive to engage with the elderly person's perspective instead of expecting them to fit into bureaucratic and professional agendas and ways of thinking* (page 47).

Narratives allow service users to tell and retell stories about their lives, and thus can be used to challenge and deconstruct dominant cultural stories that can serve to oppress them (Milner, 2001). However, much may depend on the skill of the practitioner involved in the assessment, and a consequence of greater interprofessional working may mean that the assessment is not led by a social worker, but by another professional involved in the care of the older person.

Personalisation may offer older lesbians and gay men the opportunity to make choices in the type of care they choose (Langley, 2001; Gay and Grey in Dorset, 2006). However, research by Killin (1993) points to older lesbians and gay men within the context of direct payments, which may have implications when considering a move towards personalisation and individual budgets. These issues include homophobia by employed personal assistants, or the personal assistant not adhering to the principle of confidentiality and disclosing the sexual orientation of the cared-for person.

The above developments raise the issue of training and guidance for local authority staff, health authority staff and unqualified personal assistant staff in the process of assessment and the implementation of direct payment schemes. Issues around diversity and choice require particular attention and increased consideration of the barriers faced of people who are gay or lesbian is essential to this process (Glasby and Littlechild, 2002). Research suggests that practitioners should take an individual responsibility to become aware of how older lesbians and gay men function within both gay and non-gay cultures (Jacobs et al., 1999). They need to become more informed about the realities of same-sex relationships and issues relating to being gay and growing old (Hays et al., 1997) and to become skilled at addressing clients' fears and needs. This could include having an awareness of legal realities and finding respectful providers.

The Civil Partnership Act 2004 has lessened the impact of inequality previously experienced by same-sex partners and has ensured employment and benefit rights. For many older lesbians and gay men, the lack of partnership rights has historically caused economic insecurity, a difficulty that may be pertinent for older lesbians who are among the poorest group in Britain (single women 65+). This is partly due to traditional low-paid part-time employment (Wilton, 1997); however, even full-time female workers have been disadvantaged due to unequal pay and pensions (Bayliss, 2000).

Another key issue for social work practice is linked to supporting those who may experience the death of a same-sex partner. The Gay and Grey Project (2006) highlighted a number of key issues including the impact of bereavement and grief on older lesbians and gay men, the 'invisibility' of their grief and lack of acknowledgement of the impact that loss of a same-sex partner can have. Practitioners need to develop sensitivity to the experience of bereavement for older lesbians and gay men, which can be fraught with extra difficulties as a result of disenfranchised grief, and lack of recognition of the importance of same-sex partnerships (Fenge and Fannin, 2009). The experience of homophobia and heterosexism may mean that older lesbians and gay men are particularly vulnerable during times of loss and bereavement, and as a result may not receive support appropriate to their needs.

Conclusion

Recent policy has raised the profile of older people, promoting person-centred and anti-ageist practice. However, the pervasive nature of ageism at not only the personal but cultural and structural levels (Thompson and Thompson, 2001) means that older people tend to be treated as a homogenous group. Diversity of experience is lost in stereotypical assumptions about the negative consequences of ageing, and there is a risk that those from minority groups remain hidden and forgotten.

The challenge for social work practice and research is to adopt approaches which encourage partnership with service users, to develop new knowledge and understanding for developing practice with minority groups in the twenty-first century. This requires developing sensitivity to the impact of discrimination and oppression on the lives and experiences of older lesbians and gay men, not only in the past but also in the present and in the future. A commitment to developing inclusive models of practice and research which allow individuals to have a voice in defining knowledge about them is also essential, as practising in an anti-oppressive way requires us to value difference rather than deny it.

This also links into anti-oppressive practice and the need for reflexivity which *demands that workers continually consider the ways in which their own social identity and values affect the information they gather* (Burke and Harrison, 2002, page 231). This may be particularly pertinent when working with 'invisible' minority groups, who unless agencies start to identify and work with, will remain 'hidden'. Individuals may not identify themselves due to concerns of being discriminated against further, and there may always be a silent minority.

ACTIVITIES

1 Consider the policy and practice of the agency you work in with regards to meeting the needs of older lesbians and gay men.

2 What implications might the personalisation agenda have for older lesbians and gay men?

3 This chapter has explored the experiences of older lesbians and gay men. Now select a different minority group and explore how its members are marginalised and excluded by society. For example, you could choose to explore older people from ethnic minorities, people with alcohol-related problems, or people with disabilities.

RECOMMENDED READING

Age Concern, *Planning for Later Life as a Lesbian, Gay Man, Bisexual or Transgendered Person*. Age Concern England, Information Sheet LC/8, 2003

Fannin, A., Fenge, L., Hicks, C., Lavin, N. and Brown, K. (2008) *Social Work Practice with Older Lesbians and Gay Men*. Exeter: Learning Matters

Chapter 9

People with learning difficulties – Issues of vulnerability

Chris Willetts

Introduction

People with learning disabilities feature as a small percentage of the total population (i.e. 1.5 million, DoH, 2001c) but figure highly in terms of need for support in leading ordinary lives. Yet in many respects, people with learning difficulties are among the most socially excluded and vulnerable in the UK today, and there is increasing evidence that even in the UK today, they still experience abuse, bullying and frequent challenges to their citizenship and rights. Without wishing to sound overly melodramatic, for many people with a learning difficulty, this disregard of their rights can be a matter of life or death.

This chapter will explore the vulnerability of people with learning difficulties (to exclusion, to any form of abuse, to any disregard of their rights) in a couple of key areas of citizenship: vulnerability to 'ill' health and subsequent poor healthcare, to abuse in differing forms such as bullying, 'institutionalised' neglect and abuse and exclusion in employment.

Recognising and addressing this vulnerability to exclusion, abuse and discrimination is the key theme of this chapter. It is aimed at new as well as relatively experienced practitioners and managers of services in the field of learning difficulties. Obviously there is much to be concerned about and although it is only possible in such a short chapter to identify some possible broad solutions, raising awareness of this vulnerability to exclusion, abuse and disregard is seen as a necessary first step to challenge that abuse, exclusion and discrimination by Thompson (2006) and Nzira and Williams (2009).

Firstly, in this chapter it would be useful to revisit some key concepts such as what is a learning difficulty, revisiting the concept of vulnerability and how it might apply to this group of people. It will conclude with some broad suggestions of how exclusion, abuse and disregard can be addressed and challenged, although more detailed discussion of how to address these key areas of vulnerability cannot be encompassed in such a brief chapter. Many of the sources in the reference list may be a useful next step to further explore ways to address the vulnerability of this group of people.

Vulnerability

To illustrate, there is the case of David Askew who collapsed and died outside his home in Manchester in March 2010 after suffering years of verbal and emotional abuse from local youths outside his home (BBC News, 11/3/2010). There was also the torture and murder of Andrew Gardner in 2008 (BBC News, 12/2/2010) and the case of Fiona Pilkington, who was 'driven' to take her own and her learning disabled daughter's life in October 2007, by the torment and emotional abuse inflicted by local gangs for over ten years. In this case the local police force were blamed by the inquest jury for persistently failing to protect the family from this abuse and bullying (BBC News, 29/9/2009).

A further example of how the vulnerability experienced by people with learning difficulties is a matter of life and death is that people with learning difficulties are 58 times more likely to die before the age of 50 than the general population (Hollins et al., 1998, cited in the Michael Report, 2008).

This report and others explored later on, suggest that many of the premature deaths experienced by people with learning difficulties would be preventable, with more training and raised awareness for healthcare staff, with more resources put into screening and disease detection and appropriate treatment.

Many of these failings in the healthcare system were put down to ignorance of the needs of people with learning difficulty, where too many healthcare professionals had a poor understanding of those needs, receive inadequate training to work with people with learning difficulties, and where their health needs were given a low priority. Worse still, on occasions, people with learning difficulties were not treated equally, or with respect or dignity (Michael Report, 2008).

Therefore it is argued in this chapter that people with learning difficulties are vulnerable: vulnerable to social exclusion, abuse in many forms, and to a disregard and discounting of them as people and citizens.

This is a numerically small group of people, who may have a diverse and profoundly affecting range of support needs that will likely impact on the entirety of that individual's life, and yet they have the same human rights as any other member of society. The full recognition of the equal human rights of people with learning difficulty is articulated in much law and policy: the Disability Discrimination Acts 1995 and 2005, the Human Rights Act 1998, the Mental Capacity Act 2005, the Equality Acts 2006 and 2010, and in the influential Department of Health White Paper *Valuing People: Improving Life Chances For People With Learning Disabilities For The 21st century* (DoH, 2001c). The Department of Health renewed its commitment to the rights of people with a learning difficulty in 2009 in its three-year strategy, *Valuing People Now*, after too little progress was made in the years following the publication in 2001 of the original *Valuing People* (DoH, 2009b).

It is also recognised that people with learning difficulties do also experience exclusion and discrimination in: employment and leisure opportunities (McConkey, 2007; DoH, 2009f); in having satisfying emotional and sexual relationships (McClimens and Combes, 2010); in enjoying the right to have families and in being parents (Llewellyn and McConnell, 2010); within the criminal justice system (Prison Reform Trust, 2007; DoH 2009e). However, there is insufficient space in this chapter to explore each of these issues, in addition to the many other areas where people with learning difficulties may be vulnerable to exclusion, abuse and discrimination.

People with a learning difficulty can be met in all walks of life; therefore it is incumbent on all care professionals to be familiar with this group of people, and current issues that may impact on people with a learning difficulty.

A note on terminology

The term 'learning disability' has been used since the early 1990s to define this 'client' group (Northfield, 2010). Before then, the terms 'mental sub-normality', 'mental retardation' and 'mental handicap' had been used. Today, these terms can appear derogatory.

Indeed Thompson (2006), among many others, argues that attention to labels and language is a major plank in anti-discriminatory practice. Today, Northfield (2010) identifies three terms that have become commonly used, especially in the UK: 'learning disability', 'learning difficulty' and 'intellectual' or 'developmental disability'. However, confusion can occur where the contemporary terms 'learning disability' and 'learning difficulty' are used interchangeably to describe the same 'client' group. This confusion can arise when there is uncertainty about whether the term 'learning difficulty' applies to specific learning problems such as dyslexia or dyscalculia, or whether it applies to people who have more pervasive disabilities of learning and cognitive ability, which may affect global functioning.

The term 'learning disability' sanctioned by the Department of Health is not universally supported either: many people given the label of 'learning disability' using the Department of Health definition would themselves prefer the label 'learning difficulty' (Emerson et al., 2005, Healthcare Commission, 2007b). This leaves a dilemma: should the term in common professional use ('learning disability') be used, or should we use the term preferred by many to whom such labels are applied, and use their preferred term 'learning difficulties'. Given the dilemma, the author of this chapter has chosen to adopt the term 'learning difficulty' in deference to the expressed wishes of the majority of people who live with these labels, who have to date articulated their preference.

Indeed, this highlights another problem in the use of labels: the professional care field is littered with other problematic terms: ('client', 'customer', 'service user', 'user of a service') and the author has adopted the term 'service user' with reservations, to describe people who may be potential or actual users of services. To finish any discussion of terminology, it is worth reiterating the views of Central England People First (2000) that *we should label jars, not people!*

What is learning difficulty?

Gates (2007) and Gates and Barr (2009) suggest that historically, there have been different ways of defining learning difficulty or disability. These include psychological, educational and medical explanations.

Watson (2007) and McKenzie and McAllister (2010) describe the use of medical frameworks to define learning disability. This approach treated it as a problem with medical causes, such as when someone is born with a particular chromosomal or genetically based inherited disabling condition that can be addressed though medical intervention and support, or where the baby or growing child could acquire a learning disability through such environmental factors as meningitis, encephalitis or anoxia, to name but three possible causes.

However, Watson acknowledges that this medical approach can have some value in preventative action: through improved preconceptual, ante-, peri- and post-natal care, or addressing the causes that may lead to someone developing brain injury and damage, such as through reduction of lead pollution over the past 30 years, or following the development of genetic screening and counselling.

Again, Watson also argues that there is value in understanding the medical cause and chromosomal and genetic profile of someone with a learning difficulty: to illustrate, people who are born with Trisomy 21 (an extra chromosome in pair 21, often referred to as Down syndrome), may often mouth-breathe because of physiological differences in their nose and facial structure. Therefore parents and carers supporting someone with this inheritance may anticipate that dryness of the mouth and frequent chest infections may occur because of this mouth breathing, so attention to good oral hygiene and frequent hydration will make it more comfortable for that person, and the prevention and early recognition of chest infections may be a priority for any carer of someone with Down syndrome. However, as Watson herself acknowledges: *Simply slotting someone into categories that inform treatment or aid prognosis should be avoided if we are truly to work with people in an individual and holistic manner* (Watson, 2007, page 22).

Many other attempts to define learning difficulty have focused on psychological, educational or functional and adaptive explanations. Such attempts often depend, according to Gates (2007), on measures of educational ability or attainment, using intelligence testing and the use of intelligence quotients (IQ), assessing psychological functioning for deviations from statistical and social norms (i.e. DSM IV), and thirdly, attempting to define learning disability in terms of the person's ability to perform, or not, the adaptive skills of living.

Some of the more recent definitions of learning disability reflect some, or all of these functional concepts. One such example is in the UK government's White Paper on Learning Difficulty (*Valuing People, DoH,* 2001c, page 14) where a learning difficulty *is said to include the presence of*:

> a significant deficit in understanding new or complex information in learning new skills (impaired intelligence), reduced ability to cope independently (social impairment), and where it started before adulthood and had a lasting effect on development.

They do also acknowledge within their definition *that people with a learning disability are people first and foremost, where emphasis should be on what they can do (supported), rather than what they cannot do* (DoH, 2001c, page 14).

These functional concepts of learning difficulty have been highly significant in shaping educational and support services for people with a learning difficulty, recognising that they need educational help and support with developing essential life skills.

However, Edgerton (1975, page 139) argued some time ago that we should adopt a cultural-anthropological view of learning difficulty. He argued that learning difficulty is a socially defined and constructed phenomenon. The words we use to label people and the concepts we use to define learning difficulty are part of that construction process. To illustrate, when considering 'adaptation' and 'social functioning', it is the 'non-disabled' who define adaptation, functioning and coping, by our standards and expectations: the concept of 'independence' is a non-disabled perspective (Barnes et al., 1999, Swain et al., 2004).

This view emphasises the need to explore the lived experience of people with disabilities, from their own viewpoint. Abberley (1987), Young (1990), Nolan (1999) and Haddon (2004) sought to explore the lived experience of disability. As Edgerton says, *most of us ... are sometime guilty of writing (and perhaps believing) that the mentally retarded [sic] and their lives are simpler than they really are* (Edgerton, 1975, page 139).

Therefore, simplistic and reductive constructions of learning difficulty may be equally guilty of this if we use a non-disabled perspective to define disability. The first large-scale survey of adults with learning difficulties in the UK (Emerson et al., 2005) was significant in its attempt to enable people with learning difficulties to define and describe their own experiences as people and citizens.

However, the last twenty years or so has been characterised by an emergent new paradigm for understanding disability and learning difficulties. In this view, learning disability or difficulty is not a condition of the individual. The experience of disability/difficulty is of the social restrictions in the world around them (of which physical barriers are just a part – attitudinal barriers are often more significant) and not the experience of having a handicapping condition (Swain et al., 2004, page 1). Therefore, the individual's experience of a disability/being disabled is created or reinforced in each encounter with disabling barriers, and the experience of disability is often an experience of oppression (Oliver, 1990; Hughes; 1998; Barnes and Mercer, 2006).

In 1975 Finkelstein put forward the argument that if *the physical and social world were adapted for wheelchair users, 'able bodied' people would become disabled* (Finkelstein, 2004, page 16). The same parallels could be made about people with learning difficulty in that if the world was not so technologically complex, not so based on literacy, numeracy and on academic achievement, people who were intellectually 'differently able' would experience less of a social 'handicap'. Finklelstein argued that it may be society's increasing complexity which has disabled anyone who does not meet the rigid expectations of advanced capitalism, technologisation and urbanisation. Oliver (1996, cited in Thompson, 2006, page 123) argues that *certainly it is true that disabled people have been systematically excluded from British Society: they have been denied inclusion into their society because of the existence of disabling barriers*. This adds weight to the views expressed by disabled people who so often describe their experience of exclusion and marginalisation.

According to Swain et al. (2004, page 1), these barriers to inclusion may include the following.

- Physical barriers to access and inclusion, which may include building design and transport.

- Negative and demeaning attitudes by others in society.

- The organisations and institutions, paradoxically including education, health and social care agencies, many of which might claim to be 'helping' but instead represent paternalistic, unresponsive and bureaucratic institutions.

- Language and culture which may exclude and oppress, for example the absence of positive role models of people with learning difficulties in the media, the low profile and ghettoisation of disabled people and the invisibility of the disability agenda in the media.

- The unequal power relationships that exist within society, which result in people with learning difficulties being marginalised, powerless and without a strong voice at both local and national policy and decision-making levels. However, some modest moves have been made in this direction where the last two co-national chairs of the DoH's Learning Disabilities Task Force has been a person with a learning difficulty (Nicola Smith in 2006–9, Scott Watkin since 2009), as are many of its members, and where at the local level, partnership boards of service users, working alongside professionals and policy-makers, are instrumental in shaping local policy and services.

Therefore, according to this perspective, supporting people with learning difficulties is not just about providing support where required to individual service users; it is about the social transformation that may be required to reduce and remove these barriers to inclusion and access, needing to be challenged through social action and public education.

These diverse definitions of what learning difficulty is, do not always sit easily with each other. For example, the medical and social action models are in some tension, especially as according to some (Hughes, 1998; Thompson, 2006), the medicalisation of disability has contributed one of the more oppressive discourses to defining the identity and experience of people with learning disabilities. However, as will be seen in more detail later, there is clear evidence that people with learning difficulties do experience higher rates of morbidity and mortality arising from their disability, but critics still maintain that this arises as much from unequal and inadequate access to mainstream-quality healthcare (DoH, 2001c 2009b; Mencap, 2004, 2007; Disability Rights Commission, 2006; Healthcare Commission, 2007b: the Michael Report, 2008; Health Service and Local Government Ombudsman 2009).

Numbers of people with a learning difficulty

Given that there is no easy or agreed way to define learning difficulty, it is difficult to know the precise number of people in the UK who could be classed as having a learning difficulty. This is in part because some people may have borderline intellectual or learning problems but which may manifest as difficulties in other areas of their lives, such as difficulty in finding and maintaining employment, or where significant numbers of people with borderline learning difficulties end up in the criminal justice system, where their learning difficulties may go unidentified. (Between 25 and 33 per cent of the prison population may have hidden or borderline learning difficulties – Dyslexia Institute, 2005; Prison Reform Trust, 2007; DoH, 2009e.)

The Foundation for People with Learning Disabilities (2007) offers a range of estimates that in the UK there are between 580,000 and 1,750,000 people who have mild learning difficulties and a further 230,000–350,000 people have severe learning difficulties.

However, these figures may not be accurate as any figure will depend on the selection and application of any criteria used to define learning difficulties, and assumes all people with difficulties have been detected.

Therefore it appears that there may be around 1.5 to 2 million people in the UK who have significant learning difficulty and although in some respects this may be a numerically small group of people, it represents a group who may have far-reaching and diverse support needs if they are to be enabled to fulfil their birthright as full citizens in society.

About vulnerability – In what way are people with learning difficulties vulnerable?

Phillips (1992, cited in Rogers, 1997) defines vulnerability as a *susceptibility to health problems, harm or neglect*. The Department of Health in *No Secrets* (2000), its multi-agency guidance to prevent the abuse of adults, defined a vulnerable adult as:

> *anyone over the age of 18 who is or may be in need of community care services, by reason of mental or other disability, age or illness, and who is or may be unable to take care of himself or herself, or unable to protect himself or herself against significant harm of exploitation.*

Although Naylor (2006) was critical of this definition for the fact that it did not explicitly include those not eligible or in receipt of services, it is a useful starting point to think about those people and groups that may be termed 'vulnerable'.

Factors that may make someone vulnerable to abuse may include (Naylor, 2006, pages 113–15) :

- over-compliance and dependence on a service or practitioner;

- fear of retaliation for complaining;

- no support networks outside of a service;

- social isolation;

- unable to communicate a complaint;

- practitioner/organisation factors: overwork, low pay, low status of work, and other psychological factors in the abuser.

In 2006, in the Safeguarding Vulnerable Groups Act (OPSI, 2006), a vulnerable adult is defined in very similar terms, identifying that being in receipt of, indeed dependent on, a service can create vulnerability, and particularly when that person has a disability, a mental health problem or is otherwise vulnerable because of their age.

Certainly reflecting on these lists of potential factors that may make someone vulnerable to abuse, it is clear that many of these vulnerability factors may directly apply to adults with learning difficulties, in that many of them may be receiving, indeed dependent on, services, unable to communicate any abuse or understand when abuse may have occurred, and be socially isolated. They may also, but not always, be receiving services from a low-paid, often low-status and frequently overworked community care workforce, in both health and social care settings.

Furthermore, *No Secrets* (DoH, 2000) defined a broad range of categories of potential abuse. These are:

- physical abuse;

- sexual abuse;

- psychological abuse;

- financial or material abuse;

- neglect or acts of omission;

- discriminatory abuse.

Indeed, in developing policy designed to safeguard adults, the Association of Directors of Social Services (ADSS, 2005) agreed that there are significant numbers of adults for whom abuse and disability compromise their access to safety; to the civil and criminal justice system; to victim support services; to housing; to health and social care; and to protective networks of family, friends and community.

If we accept these definitions of abuse, as well as the more obvious forms of abuse, it can be argued that people with a learning difficulty are vulnerable to, and indeed experience, discrimination and social exclusion which could neatly fall into the definitions of vulnerability outlined above. To illustrate this point, it might be useful to compare these definitions of vulnerability to abuse with definitions of discrimination, oppression and social exclusion.

Discrimination

> *... is inequality and unfairness. Power is exerted over those who are seen as different in such a way that few opportunities, few resources, less protection and fewer rights are available to them than to more powerful or higher status groups.*

> (Nzira and Williams, 2009, page 4)

Oppression

> *... oppression goes beyond discrimination, to involve a lower evaluation of the worth of individuals or groups, a rejection of them, their exclusion from valued social roles, and even a denial of the existence or a right to exist.*

> (Nzira and Williams, 2009, page 4)

Social exclusion

The Department of Communities and Local Government in 2005 defined social exclusion as being:

> *a shorthand label for what can happen when individuals or areas suffer from a combination of linked problems such as unemployment, poor skills, low incomes,*

poor housing, high-crime environments, bad health and family breakdown. It can also have a wider meaning which encompasses the exclusion of people from the normal exchanges, practices and rights of society.

It is therefore argued that people with learning difficulties can experience any of these forms of abuse, but are particularly vulnerable to discriminatory abuse, and experience discrimination, oppression and social exclusion as forms of abuse as defined in *No Secrets* (DoH, 2000) and by the ADSS (2005). It is argued in much of this chapter that people with a learning difficulty are vulnerable to, and do in fact experience this discriminatory and socially excluding abuse.

The rest of the chapter outlines areas in which people with a learning difficulty are vulnerable to this discriminatory and oppressive abuse in two key areas: in health and healthcare, as victims of disability hate crime as well as institutional abuse and neglect when receiving services.

The health of people with a learning difficulty – a disturbing tale of health inequalities

People who have a learning difficulty suffer increased health-related problems compared with the general population (Acheson, 1998; Hollins et al., 1998; NHS Scottish Executive, 2004; DoH, 2001c, 2009b). As mentioned earlier, people with learning difficulties are 58 times more likely to die before the age of 50 than the general population (Hollins et al.,1998, also cited in the Michael Report, 2008).

Coronary heart disease (CHD) is the second most common cause of death for the general population in the UK, with these figures the same in the learning disability population (Hollins et al., 1998). Respiratory disease is the leading cause of death for people with learning difficulties (Carter and Jancar, 1983; Puri et al., 1995; Holland et al., 1997, cited in Michael, 2008), and is much higher than for the general population. Equally there are much higher rates of cancer, especially gastrointestinal cancer (Cooke, 1997, cited in Michael, 2008). Death from epilepsy, especially sudden unexpected death in epilepsy (SUDEP), is highest in people with learning difficulties, particularly those with severe difficulties. The National Institute for Clinical Effectiveness (NICE, 2002, cited in Michael, 2008, page 15) estimated that 40 per cent of adult deaths from SUDEP were preventable with better informed and trained staff.

Many sources suggest that much of this ill health and premature death from all these causes is preventable to a varying but definite extent, as they may be caused by sedentary lifestyles, side-effects from medication, the lack of financial and mental resources and capability to enjoy healthy eating and more active lifestyles, especially for people with more severe difficulties who may not have access to staff and support to get out and about or eat well (Thompson and Pickering, 2001; Emerson et al., 2005; Social Care Institute for Excellence, 2005; Healthcare Commission, 2007b; Michael, 2008, DoH 2009b).

There is also evidence that people with learning difficulties experience higher rates of mental ill health than the general population. A number of prevalence studies of mental ill health in people with learning difficulties range from a study citing a figure of 11.4 per cent (Patel et al., 1993) to Enfield and Tonge (1996), who cite a figure of 40 per cent; Gilbert et al. (1986), who cite a figure of 64 per cent in children with severe disabilities, and Ballinger et al. (1991), who cite a figure of 80 per cent. Emerson et al. (2005) suggest a consensus figure that as many as 40 per cent of people using learning difficulty services have an additional mental health problem.

Matson and Sevin (1994, cited in Priest and Gibbs, 2004) and Corbett (2007) suggest that there may be many reasons why people with learning difficulties experience higher rates of mental ill health than the general population. Organic explanations suggest that people with learning difficulties may have differences in neurological structures and make-up, which may account for this difference. For example, people with Down syndrome appear to have a geater predisposition to developing Alzheimer's disease than the general population.

However, they suggest that the higher rates of mental ill health may be social-environmental and to do with the different and often abnormal and overprotected experiences of people with learning difficulties. They argue that many people with learning difficulties experience social isolation, which may cause many to develop depression; people may become aggressive due to conditioned responses in that it is often a learned means of communicating a simple human need for attention; or people with learning difficulties may have led such sheltered and isolated lives that they may suffer from anxiety from the most moderate social experience, such as extreme fear of dogs when out on the street, or other social anxiety states.

Going back to the earlier discussion of vulnerability, it is argued that these high rates of physical and mental ill health are one form of vulnerability experienced by people with learning difficulties, if one accepts Phillips' definition of vulnerability cited earlier, as a *susceptibility to health problems, harm or neglect* (Phillips 1992, cited in Rogers, 1997).

However, equally worrying is that any individual health problem experienced by people with learning difficulties is compounded by problems of poor access to quality mainstream services, where they too seldom receive proper and appropriate support with those health needs (DoH, 2001c, 2009b; Michael, 2008; Mencap, 2004, 2007; Disability Rights Commission, 2006; Healthcare Commission, 2007b; Health Service and Local Government Parliamentary Ombudsman, 2009).

Mencap, in its influential *Death By Indifference* Report (2007), highlighted the cases of six people who it claims died needlessly and in unnecessary pain and discomfort. In one case investigated by Mencap, Emma was turned away three times by her GP and local hospital, despite not eating, having a swelling in her groin, and being in a great deal of pain. On each of these three occasions she was turned away without any pain relief, and eventually died aged 26 of cancer that might have been treatable if detected earlier. Mencap concluded that the doctors and nurses did not offer treatment or pain relief in the mistaken assumption that she could not consent to treatment, or that her behaviour, which was described as 'challenging', was put down to her learning difficulties, rather than assuming that she might actually be in pain. There seemed also to be an implied assumption by the healthcare team that her quality of life and her experience of pain may not have been the same as that of a non-disabled person.

In *Death By Indifference* (Mencap, 2007), the cases of five other people they claim died needlessly are also described. Mencap concluded that this constituted systematic neglect by healthcare services to offer fair, equal and appropriate treatment to these six people, which echoed the findings of their earlier *Treat Me Right* (Mencap, 2004) investigation, and the Disability Rights Commission investigation, *Equal Treatment – Closing The Gap* (2006). Mencap went as far as calling this 'institutional discrimination' against people with learning difficulties, coining the term used in the Macpherson Report of 1999 to describe the institutional failings of the Metropolitan Police in their failure to adequately investigate the racist murder of Stephen Lawrence (Williams, 2009).

There is certainly evidence too that it's not just in mainstream primary and secondary healthcare services that the health needs of people with learning difficulties are not adequately addressed. The Healthcare Commission (2007b), the Michael Report (2008) and DoH (2009b) all found evidence that the many health needs or challenges faced by people with learning difficulties may not even be picked up adequately by their regular professional carers, who should be expected to have the necessary insights and communication skills to be aware of potential or actual health problems, especially in people with more severe learning difficulties. Again, they found that not everyone with learning difficulties had a person-centred Health Action Plan, an expectation that was originally laid out in 2001 in *Valuing People* (DoH, 2001a).

To summarise, the additional health challenges experienced by people with learning difficulties, sometimes caused by their situation and enforced, less healthy lifestyles, together with the lack of access to adequate and timely healthcare of good quality to meet their needs, constitutes a dual vulnerability. This vulnerability may be especially acute for people who have communication difficulties and need help understanding what is happening to them.

In order to address the shortcomings highlighted in the provision of healthcare for people with learning difficulty, both the Michael Report (2008) and the Health and Local Government Ombudsman Report (2009) recommended the following.

1 Ensuring that all people with a learning difficulty have good-quality health action plans in place, and that communication/health passports be used to ensure good communication of appropriate information to healthcare professionals about the service user and their needs, and the way that they might need or prefer support to be given.

2 The health needs of people with learning difficulties should represent a higher priority for the NHS.

3 There needs to be more awareness and training among commissioners of services, managers and healthcare practitioners about the health needs of people with learning difficulties, including training in how to communicate with them and anticipate and respond to their needs.

4 Compliance with the legislative framework covering disability discrimination and mental capacity should be monitored and managed more effectively in primary, community, secondary or specialist care services.

These reflect a need for a shift in attitude and a re-prioritisation so that the health needs of this vulnerable group are met in a way that anyone else would expect to have their healthcare needs met.

Abuse – victims of hate crime and victims of institutional abuse

In *Valuing People Now* (DoH, 2009b), people with learning difficulties said they have a right to live in safety and to be taken seriously when they complain about abuse or report a crime against them. According to Mencap (2009), they already should be protected against abuse and disability hate crime under the Disability Discrimination Act 1995, the Protection from Harassment Act 1997 and the Human Rights Act 1998, as well as receiving the same protection as anyone else under common and criminal law such as the Crime and Disorder Act 1998.

However, there is growing evidence of an increase in reported disability hate crime, much of it directed at people with learning difficulties. In the first national survey of adults with a learning difficulty, it was found that people with learning difficulties who responded in the survey were more likely to have reported a crime that had happened to them, than is found in the general population (Emerson et al., 2005).

The cases of David Askew (BBC News, 11/3/2010), Andrew Gardner (BBC News, 12/2/2010) and Fiona Pilkington (BBC News, 29/9/2009), who were all victims of disability hate crime, were mentioned earlier. In the first national survey of adults with learning difficulties undertaken in 2003–4, Emerson et al. (2005) found:

> One in three people (32%) said they did not feel safe either in their homes, their local area or using public transport. Nearly one in three people (32%) said someone had been rude or offensive to them in the last year because they have learning difficulties. Nearly one in ten people (9%) said they had been the victim of crime in the last year. People with learning difficulties were less likely to be a victim of crime than other people, but they were slightly more likely to be attacked.

(Emerson et al., 2005, page 6)

Although there is no explicit legal definition of disability hate crime, the Crown Prosecution Service (CPS) adopt the following definition: *Any criminal offence, which is perceived, by the victim or any other person, to be motivated by hostility or prejudice based on a person's disability or perceived disability* (CPS, 2009).

Further media evidence of possible disability hate crime is coming to light, for example, in reports on Disability Now online hate crime dossier of personal accounts covering 2006–7 (Disability Now, 2010; BBC News online, 19/8/2008; BBC News online Spotlight on Disability Hate Crime, 29/9/2009; The Independent online, 9/12/2009, Tom Shakespeare in the *Guardian*, 12/3/2010; and various personal accounts on Mencap – *Hate Crime, Real Life Stories*, 2010). This quite clearly reflects that people with disabilities and learning difficulties are, as in the words of Tom Shakespeare, vulnerable to abuse, ridicule and attack.

In addition to the vulnerability to being a victim of disability hate crime, Higgins (2006) and Samuel (2009) found a worryingly low rate of prosecution of disability hate crimes. The government responded to the growing incidence of disability hate crime and in 2008, the Home Office funded a joint publication with Inclusion North, called *Learning Disability Hate Crime: Good Practice Guidance for Crime and Disorder Reduction*. This guidance defines hate crime, sets out key findings from the original research on the prevalence and possible causes of disability hate crime and provides guidance on how to gather information, promote independence and safety, and support victims, witnesses and survivors of hate crime.

The exact causes of disability hate crime are complex and multi-factored and its recent rise is currently being investigated. However, some of the factors mentioned earlier that Naylor (2006) identified that make some adults vulnerable, make people with learning difficulties likely targets for abuse as the victims of crime, such as their social isolation so that they may rarely have close family and friends to speak up for them, who could offer support when they are targeted. They may also have poor communications ability. In the case of bullying, the fear of retaliation if they make a complaint can keep an individual locked into a vicious cycle of bullying and abuse.

Again, a dual vulnerability is apparent when the original bullying and abuse are compounded and amplified by the failure of the authorities to either act decisively to protect the victims, as in the cases of David Askew or Fiona Pilkington's, or when the authorities fail to prosecute hate crime offences, as admitted by both the Crown Prosecution Service and Association of Chief Police Officers (Higgins, 2006; Home Office and Inclusion North, 2008; and Samuel, 2009).

As well as these factors identified by Naylor contributing to the vulnerability of people with learning difficulties to hate crime, these very same factors, in addition to a potential or actual dependence on service providers, can make adults with learning difficulties vulnerable to institutional neglect, abuse and abusive treatment by paid and professional carers and by services.

In July 2006, The Healthcare Commission (since replaced by the Care Quality Commission) issued a report into the abuse and neglect of people with learning difficulties receiving services in Cornwall Partnership NHS Trust, following a joint investigation with the Commission for Social Care Inspection (CSCI). The investigation reported that:

> *some individuals ... have suffered abuse including physical, emotional and environmental abuse ... that some people using its services have had to endure years of abusive practices and some have suffered real injury as a result.*

Further, the investigation discovered that one person

> *spent 16 hours a day tied to their bed or wheelchair, for what staff wrongly believed was for that person's own protection ... More than two-thirds of the sites visited placed unacceptable restrictions on people living there.*

For example, they lived behind locked internal and external doors to restrict their movement, and taps and light fittings had been removed. There was also the excessive use of physical restraint and the overuse of discretionary 'PRN as required' medication to 'calm' service users. Institutional neglect was widespread so that few service users had community care assessments or up-to-date person-centred plans.

Within six months of this report being published, the Healthcare Commission published another report (January, 2007a), this time into the abuse of people with learning difficulties at the Sutton and Merton Primary Care Trust. They found:

> *that the model of care was largely based on the convenience of the service providers rather than the needs of individuals. For example, during meal times some people's shoulders were wrapped in a large sheet of blue tissue paper, and they were then fed at a speed that would not allow for any enjoyment of the food.*

They also discovered that the overall provision of activities was very low, with some people having only three to four hours of activity a week. Again there was an excessive use of inappropriate restraint, and worryingly, they investigated 15 serious incidents of sexual and physical abuse, including one incident when a woman with learning difficulties was raped. In both the cases of Cornwall Partnership Trust, and Sutton and Merton PCT, the Healthcare Commission found that a double vulnerability existed. The existence of neglect and abuse, arising through a lack of training and supervision, accompanied by low staff morale, was equally compounded and amplified by the management's failure of leadership to set high standards and to then monitor care quality and to act to address any shortcomings or less than good practice.

In response to these two cases of institutional abuse in learning difficulty services coming in quick succession, the Healthcare Commission committed to carrying out a national audit of specialist inpatient healthcare services for people with learning difficulties in England. The subsequent report, *A Life Like No Other* (Healthcare Commission, 2007b), was published later the same year, and although to some extent based on some level of service self-report/self-evaluation, was backed up with questionnaires, interviews conducted with service users and institutional visits. Disturbingly, despite some cases of good practice, it found that the institutional abuse and neglect discovered in Cornwall, and in Sutton and Merton were not isolated cases at all. In six services, they had serious concerns about safety. These concerns were followed up immediately so that the necessary improvements were made without delay.

They found only a few services where the quality of care and the attention paid to the safety of people with learning difficulties were uniformly good across all aspects of care. At most, many provided for the basic level of care need only. They discovered a lack of person-centred plans across many of the services visited, where stimulating activities were rarely provided, and where environments were often described as poor and unhomely. Again the dual vulnerability existed where neglect and the lack of good care and support were compounded by the lack of leadership, monitoring and lack of attention to safeguarding issues (Healthcare Commission, 2007b).

The Commission set out a number of performance indicators that are an attempt to benchmark best practice, and there is an expectation that the management of each service visited will respond with an action plan to monitor these indicators as well as respond to any shortcomings or concerns highlighted in the audit process of that particular service.

These indicators include the expectation that every service user will have up-to-date, person-centred life and health plans, with procedures for safeguarding adults (and children when services are offered to children) in place and monitored. They proposed the extension of advocacy services and an invitation was extended to a local Learning Difficulty Partnership Board to take up external scrutiny of local services. They also recommended an acceleration of the NHS Campus closure so that people with learning difficulties could live in their own homes wherever possible and that only high-quality, specialist NHS service for people with the most complex or challenging needs would remain.

In response to the publication of *A Life Like No Other* (Healthcare Commission, 2007a), the House of Lords and House of Commons Joint Committee on Human Rights published *A Life Like Any Other? Human Rights of Adults with Learning Disabilities* (House of Commons, 2008). This was a restatement of the need to respect the human rights of people with learning difficulties.

However, given the need to listen to the views and wishes of people with learning difficulty scheduled for moving into their own homes, it is important as the last few NHS Campuses close in 2010–11, that service users are given sufficient time, support and scope to articulate their views and wishes about the process and to have those views and wishes taken into due account in the process. This concern is explicitly noted by the Joint Lords and Commons Report following evidence to the Committee that this is not always the case (House of Commons, 2008, page 30).

The government's response to the Healthcare Commission Reports was outlined in *Valuing People Now*, and the resulting *Valuing People Now: The Delivery Plan* intended to guide services to meet the targets set (DoH, 2009g). In it they restate their commitment to the four key principles outlined in the 2001 *Valuing People* White Paper: *Rights: Independent Living: Choice and Control: Inclusion*. To this end, such as in the area of promoting employment, the DoH have published a supplementary strategy, *Valuing Employment Now* (DoH, 2009f) to promote employment as means of achieving control and inclusion for people with a learning difficulty who can and want to have paid employment.

However, given the lack of progress in delivering the vision contained in the 2001 *Valuing People*, especially given that other service-user groups have had their own National Service Framework, the lack of 'teeth' behind the Valuing People/Valuing People Now agenda must give some cause for pessimism. A recent change of government in 2010 and the much-vaunted public-sector squeeze that may accompany the national economic difficulties of 2009–10 must be further causes for pessimism.

Conclusion

From the discussion above, a strong case can be made, using the definitions of vulnerability and vulnerable adult given earlier, that people with learning difficulty constitute a very vulnerable group of people indeed. As well as their vulnerability to more obvious forms of neglect and abuse such as physical, sexual, financial and emotional abuse, it is hoped that the case has been made that people in difficulty often experience discriminatory abuse too.

For some, whether receiving poor and inadequate healthcare, or when being a victim of disability hate crime, this vulnerability may be a matter of life or death or lead them to being vulnerable at least to serious harm or hurt.

The human rights of people with learning difficulties are clearly articulated in much of the policy and law mentioned above. However, it is quite clear, as Thompson recommends (2006), that occasionally we may need to use that law and policy to bring to account not only the perpetrators of abuse, but also the managers and service providers, whether these be doctors, police officers, professional carers or service managers, who fail to implement policies to safeguard adults from any type of abuse whether it be physical, emotional or institutional abuse.

The failure to act seriously to challenge the discriminatory and institutional abuse faced by people with learning difficulties adds weight to the social model of disability perspective, in that vulnerability does not inevitably arise out of a person's genetic inheritance or health identity, but in the way that others, and how society as a whole, treats and values that group of people. This is their social handicap.

Valuing People Now (DoH, 2009b) restated the government's commitment to a rights-based agenda, to promote valued and equal life opportunities for people with a learning difficulty. However, this group of people remain vulnerable while we do too little to support and uphold their human rights to live free of abuse and discrimination.

Chapter 10

Safeguarding adults for community care

Linda Naylor

Introduction

There has been a rapid development of work in the area of adult protection or safeguarding adults in the past ten years, and it now occupies a central position in any work with vulnerable adults. Despite the fact that the first government guidance to local authorities and their partners did not appear until 2000 (DoH, 2000), many areas were by then already well advanced in the work of protecting vulnerable adults. *No Secrets* in 2000 took this a stage further by requiring that all local authorities have a multi-agency policy by October 2001. As with many good initiatives, one of the main difficulties with this was the lack of any additional funds to accompany it. Many multi-agency policies are led strongly by one agency, with the others showing less commitment.

The Association of Directors of Social Services (2005) issued guidance on safeguarding adults which was an attempt to streamline and set standards for adult protection for local authorities. These recommendations have partially been implemented but had no statutory force. The guidance did trigger a shift away from adult protection towards safeguarding adults, reflecting a similar change in child protection. From 2001 onwards, there has been concern about the great variations in local adult protection policies even in adjacent areas. In October 2008 there was a consultation to review *No Secrets* and look at its weaknesses. This review posed questions about the term 'vulnerable adult' with discussion about replacing it with 'person at risk'. Currently the local authority leads the process and this is debated with the review. The review also discussed the need for legislation and an outcomes framework linked to national guidance to gain more consistency. The reponses to the *No Secrets* review were issued in July 2009 and service users were clear in saying that the victims' voice must not be lost and they wished to retain control in relation to decisions about protection. The government response was very limited – to legislate in the future for Safeguarding Adults Boards and to consider national guidance.

Adult protection has followed a slow evolutionary process. Initially, there was a lot of interest in two separate fields. Firstly, in the 1970s, the physical abuse of older people hit the headlines with such phrases as 'granny bashing' (Baker, 1975). Formal recognition of elder abuse in Britain arose in 1993 with Department of Health guidelines (1993). In a completely separate development in the same year (Brown and Turk, 1993), the issue of the sexual abuse of adults with learning disabilities became the focus of attention. There was little recognition of the other areas of abuse until the mid-1990s when additional categories were at least noted. As with child protection, attention was focused on particular types of abuse, and the others not always acknowledged. In addition, the focus was on learning disability and older people, not the whole range of vulnerable adults.

Defining adult abuse

The first definition that is important is defining who are vulnerable adults, and who therefore fall within protective policies. DoH (2000) adopted the Law Commission definition as follows:

> *anyone of 18 years and over who is or may be in need of community care services by reason of mental or other disability, age or illness and who is or may be unable to take care of himself or herself, or unable to protect himself or herself against significant harm or serious exploitation.*

There have been some discussions about changing this definition to include those not eligible for services. ADSS (2005) proposed widening the scope of policies to include safeguarding adult citizen rights. The Law Commission review currently favours the term 'adults at risk'.

The difficulties of defining safeguarding adults parallel the historical development cited. Many early definitions were specific to the abuse of older people and did not serve any wider function for other adult client groups. Terms like 'elder abuse' were not helpful in this respect. Finkelhor and Pillemer (1988) spoke of *definitional array* with no generally accepted term for elder abuse at that point. Action on Elder Abuse (1995) adopted the following definition:

> *Elder abuse is a single or repeated act or lack of appropriate action, occurring within any relationship where there is an expectation of trust, which causes harm or distress to an elder person.*

There was a gradual broadening to create a definition which included all vulnerable adult groups, culminating in the *No Secrets* definition (DoH, 2000):

> *Abuse is a violation of an individual's human and civil rights by any other person or persons.*

This definition is very broad and includes any rights issue with no limiting factor of harm being caused. It is therefore not a functional definition which agencies can use to determine which cases to respond to as abuse, and which to investigate. As in child protection, there is a need to define the categories of abuse and thresholds for action to guide local decision-making. Often, it is not the category of abuse that challenges staff but the threshold for taking action. At what point should staff refer the matter on to social services for investigation? Very few multi-agency policies discuss this issue, although some guidance by Brown and Stein (1998) suggests such factors as individual frailty, the effect of the abuse, and risk of repetition being taken into account.

Categories of abuse have again expanded as awareness has grown. Initial emphasis on the physical and financial abuse of the elderly (Lau and Kosberg, 1979) was perpetuated in most studies of older people abuse. Much of the work on learning disability emphasised sexual abuse. However, there is a real attempt in *No Secrets* to be both generic and also broad in categorisation with the use of the categories:

- physical abuse;
- sexual abuse;
- psychological abuse;
- financial or material abuse;
- neglect and acts of omission;
- discriminatory abuse.

Vulnerability and context

There are a number of factors which make certain adults vulnerable to abuse. In looking at these, it is important to remember that all these factors could be present and the contexts allow for abuse, but it needs an abuser for abuse to take place. It is not the responsibility of the vulnerable adult that they are abused. There is a danger in seeing certain groups of adults as necessarily and automatically frail and vulnerable.

One vulnerability factor is over-compliance, where vulnerable adults are used to having little say in services and accepting whatever treatment comes their way. This can lead to a lack of resistance to poor treatment or abuse. An absence of wider social networks can create isolation, leaving some people easy prey to abusers and unlikely to speak out if they are abused. Some will be dependent on their abuser for basic survival and fear retaliation. The victim may blame themselves for the abuser's behaviour or feel protective towards them. Many vulnerable adults have poor access to non-specialist services, and although they have a range of services specific to their disability, do not know how to access the police and more routine help (Williams, 1995). Many adults with learning or physical disability have limited sexual knowledge, despite attempts in recent years to counter this. Older people can also lack the confidence to describe sexual matters due to a particular generational view of the subject. Some vulnerable adults need help with their personal care which gives more people access to them and the heightened possibility of abuse. It can also make it harder for someone to be sure that it is abuse they are receiving.

Any communications limitation makes adults more vulnerable because of their limited methods of 'speaking out' if something happens to them. Sometimes, the only way for them to show something untoward has happened is by their behaviour. These behaviours can then be labelled as 'challenging' rather than recognising the cause. In both older people and people with learning disability, multiple disabilities seem to create greater vulnerability to abuse (Brown and Turk, 1992).

For some vulnerable adults, particularly those with dementia, mental illness or learning disability, confusion can be blamed for disclosures, and therefore appropriate action may not be taken. A significant case in this respect was *R(B) v DPP 09,* where a man's past mental health was not seen as a good reason for a case not going to trial when he was physically assaulted. The court stated that the credibility of a person as a witness cannot be based on assumptions due to past mental health problems.

In the area of sexual abuse, there is the additional factor of the behaviour of sexual abusers and the links with the vulnerability of the adults involved. There is limited research, but it appears that some of the grooming and insidious build-up present in the sexual abuse of children is also present with adults. It is possible that such abusers pick certain groups of vulnerable adults because they will make poor witnesses in court and these groups would have had little chance of getting into court until recent changes were made.

There has been a general assumption that a significant proportion of domestic abuse is related to carer stress. Homer and Gilleard (1990) characterised the abuser as male or female with alcohol problems. In their research, 45 per cent of carers admitted to one form of abuse and most were spouses or children. The emphasis on 'stressed carers' has been challenged by Bennett and Kingston (1993) as promoting a 'victim mentality'. The presence of disruptive behaviour in the elderly victim and the poor quality of early relationships are the strongest predictors of abuse (Biggs et al., 1995). Kappeler (1995) suggests that in a society based on exchange relationships, those with nothing to exchange for their care are more likely to be victimised. Cooper et al. (2009) undertook a small-scale study of people with dementia living at home and found that 52 per cent of carers reported some abusive behaviour, 34 per cent significant abusive behaviour towards the person they looked after. Verbal abuse was the commonest but 1.4 per cent reported physical abuse.

There has been a wealth of information published about indicators, or signs and symptoms of abuse. While these can lead to a false optimism about spotting abuse, when used with caution they can help workers be more aware. Some lists are category specific, although a high level of overlap is acknowledged (Breckman and Adelman, 1988). Most agencies now include such lists in their policies and they are increasingly generic rather than specific to one adult client group.

Incidence

The difficulties of defining abuse make it challenging to be clear about its incidence. Aggregate data cannot be discussed as each survey has defined abuse in a different way. Estimates will also be based on reported incidents which by no means reflect the whole position. The Action on Elder Abuse study (2006) has added to our understanding of the reporting of incidents of abuse to local authorities with a monitoring study. Very few referrals are made by the public. Referrals came from social services (13.6 per cent), service providers (14.2 per cent), family (4.9 per cent) and the vulnerable adult (5.9 per cent). The most common form of abuse was physical (33.8 per cent) followed by neglect.

Among the concern about the sexual abuse of adults with learning disability, it is easy to lose sight of the very common stories told by practitioners about the financial abuse of this group. Bewley (1997) shows how little amount of control many people with a learning disability have over their money and possessions. Assumptions that are often made (i.e. that people are incapable) mean that real choice about finance is not available; there are also more extreme cases of abuse.

Incidence figures for the sexual abuse of those with learning disability are readily available although now dated. The major research in this area was by Brown, et al. (1995), who estimated that there would be 1,200 new cases of serious sexual abuse of adults with learning disability per year. A Mencap study (2000) showed that 32 per cent of people with learning disability were bullied daily or weekly and 23 per cent were physically assaulted.

For older people, Pritchard (1995) undertook extensive research in Britain and concluded that between 5 and 10 per cent of older people suffer some form of abuse. Aitken and Griffin (1996) concluded from her research that financial abuse was so commonplace that workers did not recognise it as an area of concern. The UK study of the abuse and neglect of older people (O'Keefe et al., 2007) have given a much fuller picture. The researchers asked about physical, emotional, financial, sexual and neglect since age 65 and in the past year. The study focused on older people living in private households and 3.8 per cent women and 1.1 per cent men reported abuse in the past year. Mistreatment increased with declining health. The study found 51 per cent of perpetrators were partners and 13 per cent care workers.

There is little research into the abuse of physically disabled adults. Simanowitz (1995) found that in his small sample of adults with either physical or learning disability:

- 50 per cent had experienced violence or harassment;
- 46 per cent had experienced psychological abuse in the past year.

Also in the past year:

- 21 per cent had experienced physical abuse;
- 14 per cent neglect;
- 10 per cent medical abuse;
- 7 per cent financial abuse.

There was a low response rate in this research, and perhaps those that responded were the disabled adults with the most concern about abuse.

Action for Blind People (2008), looking at partially sighted and blind people, found they were four times more likely to experience physical or verbal abuse than other adults and half as likely to go to the police as they felt they would not be taken seriously. Of the respondents 54 per cent said they had been abused by a stranger, 6 per cent by a partner, 7 per cent by a family member and 4 per cent by a friend.

For adults with mental health problems, the limited research reflects the myth perpetuated in the media that they are a risk to the public rather than being at risk in any way themselves. Wienhardt, Bickham and Carey (1999) stated that women with severe mental illness had an increased risk of being sexually coerced, and in their sample 13 per cent of female outpatients had been forced into sex against their will in the past two months.

The intrinsic problem with assessing the level of abuse in mental health services is that what service users say is often seen as part of their condition rather than a credible account of a real experience. Some studies suggest a high level of risk for inpatients; for example, the National Patient Safety Agency (2005) described 122 sexual incidents and 11 alleged rapes by staff on mental health wards in England and Wales over a two-year period. Mind (2007) found 71 per cent respondents had been victims of crime or harassment over a two-year period. This included 22 per cent who had been physically assaulted (3.6 per cent British Crime Survey (BCS)) 10 per cent sexually assaulted (BCS <1 per cent); 41 per cent of the respondents described ongoing bullying, with only 19 per cent feeling safe in their home all of the time. One in three had told no one, which challenges adult protection in the area of mental health.

There have been a number of inquiry reports into institutional abuse that are often in relation to concerns about a specific residential setting (for example, Gibbs et al., 1987). Some of these reports have emphasised the corruption factor of one individual, the 'bad apple' hypothesis, which is an inadequate explanation for abusive cultures (Wardhaugh and Wilding, 1993). Manthorpe et al. (1999) said that many approaches to institutional abuse tend to focus on individual workers with the idea of flushing out the individual to solve the problem. Common themes emerge from the inquiry reports, with abuse seen as resulting from lack of staff training, professional isolation, stress, low morale, organisational culture, personal characteristics of both victims and perpetrators and a lack of adequate resources. The reluctance of clients to make complaints, and the stifling of them, mean that institutional abuse can go unrecognised. The misuse of restraint and the lack of policies around the sexuality of service users also contributes.

In recent years the key institutional abuse inquiries have been in relation to adults with learning disability. In Cornwall the Healthcare Commission found people with multiple injuries, restrained and their movement restricted. There was a lack of personal possessions and clothing, with understimulation. Medication was administered covertly. There was little encouragement to independence and complaints handling was poor. Many residents had not chosen where to live and some had not received community care assessments. Staff in the provider trust were aware of reporting arrangements but did not define what they were seeing as abuse. There was also criticism of internal investigations by provider managers rather than impartial investigations by the local authority.

Soon after, there were similar concerns coming to light in Sutton and Merton PCT with the care of adults with learning disability. This was outmoded institutional care which the trust had tried to close down but faced relatives' objections. There was neglect and an average of 3–4 hours' stimulation per person per week. The inspectors were invited in as there were concerns about 15 serious incidents of abuse in three years. Person-centred planning was not happening and there was inappropriate use of restraint. Care seemed to be based on the needs of the institution, not the individual, with set mealtimes and a lack of cultural awareness. There was insufficient integration into the community and very little advocacy or complaints processes.

There have been fewer research studies devoted to institutional abuse, and the emphasis has largely been on domestic abuse. Decalmer and Glendenning (1997) suggested that the most common abuse is institutional abuse, where the environment and practices of the institution become abusive in themselves. Wardhaugh and Wilding (1993) suggested that the depersonalisation of the institution allows for the viewing of individuals as less than human, which creates a climate for abuse.

Training programmes are often used to address institutional abuse, with the assumption being that increased training will prevent future abuse. Taylor and Dodd (2003) showed in their research that the effectiveness of training may be variable: 75 per cent of the research sample had received training on abuse but there remained a culture of acceptance of the service user to user abuse which was not always taken as seriously. Staff in this study seemed to make their own judgements about reporting and 35 per cent would only report an abuse incident if they themselves considered the abuse severe enough; 75 per cent of staff would only report the abuse if there was concrete evidence; and 20 per cent were hesitant to report an abuse allegation that may not be true. Some 20 per cent were reluctant to report abuse if it were breaking the service user's confidentiality. The handling of allegations against staff was concerning, with 10 per cent reluctant to report if the alleged perpetrator was a staff member – 30 per cent would discuss the concerns with the staff member first, which could destroy evidence.

An additional concern is how effectively institutional abuse is investigated. The roles of the Care Quality Commission (CQC), the police and social services are not always clear in local policies. The roles of agencies in institutional abuse vary around the country and are often *ad hoc* and confused. The CQC protocol has helped to clarify their role but the organisational changes they have experienced have made consistent joint working challenging.

Links with other family violence

It is important to place safeguarding adults in the context of some related areas while not losing the emphasis that not all adult abuse happens in the home setting. There are links with domestic violence, and O'Keefe et al. (2007) confirm that elder abuse is often spouse abuse. Some of the abuse that takes place against vulnerable adults is in the form of domestic violence (i.e. an older couple where one partner has always been violent to the other and they are now vulnerable and frail). The cycle of violence has also been recognised in some families where violent acts have been perpetrated within families, and some of it in the form of adult abuse. However, there is a danger that physical abuse is emphasised at the expense of the other categories of abuse where links are made with domestic violence.

In *No Secrets*, there is no mention of domestic violence despite recent guidance. This separation of the two interrelated areas is a significant shortfall in practice. Domestic violence is not always a feature of adult abuse, but the vulnerability of the adults should always be considered in domestic violence situations.

There are very significant theoretical links with child protection. Clearly, there are also huge differences – not least that adults have the rights and choices of adults, and are not protected by child care legislation which assumes children lack capacity and need protection. Despite the progressive proposals in *Who Decides?* there is still no emergency protective legislation for adults that is equivalent to the Emergency Protection Orders in the Children Act 1989. The adult is presumed in law to have the right to make their own decisions and there are very limited powers to interfere with these. The Mental Capacity Act 2005 gives some powers where an adult lacks capacity but there are limited options for the capacitated adult.

Stevenson (1996) discusses the over-proceduralisation of child protection and the dangers of this happening in adult protection. The emphasis on risk and the desire to simplify the process of decision-making has some important lessons for adult protection. Stevenson also discusses the danger of protection being split off from wider welfare issues, which has caused the need for refocusing in child protection and could happen again in adult protection. Safeguarding-adults work needs to be set within a wider framework of needs assessment and care management. Currently, the pressure of work with increasing refer-rals for safeguarding adults is leading to many local authorities considering setting up specialist units. Although there would be some benefits in terms of specialist knowledge, this could lead to an overemphasis on protection and a lack of recognition of prevention and wider planning.

There are other obvious learning points from Local Safeguarding Childrens Boards for Safeguarding Adults Boards formed as the result of *No Secrets*. Stevenson (1996) has stressed that inter-agency co-operation is just as crucial in safeguarding adults as it is with children. Every child death inquiry from Maria Colwell (1974) onwards has accentuated the need for good inter-agency communication and this is as true in safeguarding adults. The effect of *No Secrets* is limited compared with the much more prescriptive *Working Together to Safeguard Children* (DoH, 2010) and all the bulk of previous guidance. It has taken many years to get certain professional groups working together to protect children and it will be a slow task in the field of safeguarding adults. This will not be helped by the lack of funding in adult protection work and the relative newness of the area to most agencies. There remains a much stronger statutory footing and clearer guidance for safe-guarding children compared with adults.

Intervention

As a result of *No Secrets*, many authorities are now giving staff training in investigating the abuse of vulnerable adults, although it is often shorter and less rigorous than the training given to childcare workers. Until recently, there was a tendency for staff in adult services to emphasise the welfare side of abuse. Faced with an abusive situation, more support services would be arranged, avoiding sometimes the confrontation of the abuser. Adult protec-tion conferences and criminal action would be far from any plans. Action on Elder Abuse (2006) showed that less than 1 per cent of the referrals were proceeding to prosecution. Pritchard (1990) described a range of services that were offered in order to help victims rather than encouraging a legal response. The emphasis on avoiding disruption and con-frontation, while motivated from a commitment to the perceived welfare of the vulnerable adult, has left some older people in unreasonable situations. It also has left the abuser free to move on and abuse elsewhere. Biggs (1996) stated that the use of care management as a response closes off other options. It leads to an emphasis on domestic abuse and solving the problem by dealing with carer-stress through more support. The carer-stress hypothesis is more comfortable for us and normalises abuse. Breckman and Adelman (1988) advocated a clear goal of an abuse-free life for the victim, and if necessary separation from the abuser to achieve this. However, the lack of an integrated view of intervention can go against this goal. There is a need for workers to see legal action and the provision of services as two of several viable options to safeguard the victim. Clough (1995) said that the two major principles should be maximum autonomy and minimum intervention.

This style of working sits uneasily alongside more joint working with the police. Social workers have not always felt confident in dealing with abuse in a manner which does not prejudice the future possible use of the criminal justice system. When social workers deal with investigation without involving the police, forensic evidence can easily be lost and the possibility of criminal action adversely affected.

There is a similar gap in working with medical colleagues, and often investigations have not included the consideration of a full medical assessment. The specialist role of the paediatrician in child protection has no similar parallel in adult protection, and any knowledge and skills are spread thinly across specialisms.

An example where intervention failed is the case of Steven Hoskins. He was a 39-year-old with learning disability and all the services failed to prevent his death in 2006 at the hands of three young adults who emotionally, physically and financially abused him in his own home. They finally forced him over a viaduct where he dropped to his death with many injuries already on his body from sustained assaults. One of Steven's attackers, Darren, was well known to services and considered to pose a risk of harm to his children. When he moved in with Steven the police warned housing officers not to visit the home alone as Darren posed such a risk. There were many missed opportunities to intervene and save Steven's life. He had expressed concerns and fears to social services, the police, a hospital and store detectives. None of these had seen it as their role to make an adult protection referral. As in so many child protection cases, the inquiry concluded there was no lack of information – all that was needed was for this all to be put together. The report said: *it is important that adult protection is triggered when someone is believed to be at risk of harm, not only at the point where there is demonstrable evidence of harm*. This case highlights how challenging it is for all agencies to recognise, respond and act on adult protection issues.

There has often been a lack of clarity about which stage of the response process staff are working within. This can lead to the wrong people acting without the appropriate skills. In the AIMS pack (2001), the distinct phases of referring, alerting and investigating are very useful in delineating the process. Many policies are now beginning to state that only suitably trained staff should work at investigation level.

The role of multi-agency conferences is not always clear in safeguarding adults. Most policies include such a meeting, but these can range from low-profile chats about clients, to conferences along the lines of child protection with rigorous procedures. Staff are often unclear about the difference between strategy meetings and conferences. Action on Elder Abuse (2006) demonstrated an under-use of conferences. The value of a clear shared protection plan cannot be overemphasised. Pritchard (1996) said that protection plans must be developed, implemented and reviewed regularly. Recent CQC inspections of local

1

authority adult services have emphasised this; for example, Poole Borough Council April 2009 where weak protection planning was criticised. Pritchard (1999) quoted two vulnerable adults who said:

> *All hell broke loose. People came to talk to me for weeks on end. Then, nothing. I thought they were going to help me. Fat chance. Things are just as they were.*

It is important that the end goal of any intervention is to improve the situation of the vulnerable adult.

Legal framework

The legal framework is significant despite the reluctance of many abused vulnerable adults to accept the legal alternative, due to fear or concern for the abuser's future. This has often led to legal remedies failing to be considered, which is very different from practice in domestic violence. There have been a number of recent changes in the law. The Mental Health Act 1983 was updated with the Mental Health Act 2007 and gives powers of access to approved mental health practitioners if the person is not 'under proper care', and offers protection to the mentally disordered from wilful neglect or ill-treatment by carers, with a power of removal via a magistrate.

Who Decides (Lord Chancellor's Department, 1997) had proposed radical changes with the introduction of emergency powers for incapacitated adults, but these were not taken forward in further guidance (Lord Chancellor's Department, 1999). Many of the other proposals were taken up in the Mental Capacity Act 2005 but there has not been an addition of emergency powers. This is currently being reconsidered in the Law Commission Review.

The issue of mental capacity is critical in deciding action in adult protection. There is a presumption that everyone has mental capacity until the contrary is proved. In undertaking investigations, capacity to consent is a key issue. There are two key capacity issues and the first is the capacity of the adult to consent to the sexual act or other act about which there is concern. If the adult has capacity and consented to the 'abusive' act, it is unlikely that any prosecution can take place although the police should still be consulted. A vulnerable adult's capacity may fluctuate over time. This can be critical in determining whether an act is abusive or consenting. The second key area where capacity is significant is consent to the process of the investigation – active involvement of the police, interviews and medical assessment. If the vulnerable adult lacks capacity for this function, it is inappropriate for their consent to the process to be sought. However, they should be engaged with the process in any way possible and a best-interests decision made. If the adult has capacity and declines assistance and refuses an investigation, actions will be limited. Such situations should be discussed at an Adult Protection Conference to ensure all agencies are aware of the risks and the danger signals.

In assessing capacity, it is important to distinguish between capacity to make the decision and the ability to communicate the decision. The Mental Capacity Act 2005 makes clear that a functional approach to capacity must be taken and the adult must be assessed in relation to their capacity for this specific decision, not a general assessment. The test is whether the person is capable of understanding the particular decision. If a particular decision is trivial, a low degree of understanding will suffice. The more complex the decision, the greater understanding is needed.

The Mental Capacity Act has set the following five key principles which make it clear that a person should be seen as having capacity unless proven otherwise.

- A person must be assumed to have capacity unless it is established he lacks capacity.
- A person is not to be treated as unable to make decisions unless all practicable steps to help him to do so have been taken without success.
- A person is not to be treated as unable to make a decision merely because he makes an unwise decision.
- An act done, or decision made, under this Act for or on behalf of a person who lacks capacity must be done or made in his best interests.
- Before the act is done, or the decision made, regard must be had to whether the purpose for which it is needed can be as effectively achieved in a way that is less restrictive of the person's rights and freedom of action.

Someone is unable to make a decision for himself if they are unable:

- to understand the information relevant to the decision;
- to retain the information;
- to use or weight that information as part of the process of making the decision;
- to communicate his decision by any means.

There is a best-interests checklist for people acting on behalf of others. The Act has extended the Court of Protection's role to cover welfare matters, not just financial matters. Lasting Power of Attorney replaces the Enduring Power of Attorney but can specify other decisions on wider welfare matters as well as finance. Most day-to-day informal decisions will be able to be taken without interference of the court with a general authority resting on the carer. The court can appoint deputies who would help with welfare and financial decisions where the person lost capacity without appointing a Lasting Power of Attorney. This replaces the previous system of receivership covering financial decision-making and extends it to include health and welfare. The Act has increased the Court of Protection's role in disputed decision-making about best interests and mental capacity. The Act has created Independent Mental Capacity Advocates to support those lacking capacity who have no one else to speak for them when decisions are taken about serious medical treatment or long-term residential care or adult protection action.

In general, the Human Rights Act 1998 has created some interesting challenges in the field of adult protection, leaving public authorities open to criticism either for failing to act to protect people from degrading or inhuman treatment or acting in a way which interferes with private and family life. Care in using correct procedures and gaining legal advice has resulted from this, and that has to be beneficial to vulnerable adults. The Data Protection Act 1998 has caused appropriate concern about the sharing of personal information, but it has to be remembered that information can still be shared where it is for the prevention or detection of a crime or to protect the vital interests of the subject of the data, even without the subject's consent. The Crime and Disorder Act 1998 Section 115 offers support to the practice of limited and responsible sharing of information in the joint agency process of detecting and preventing offences to victims. The Act means that disclosing information where this is necessary or expedient in preventing crime is still legal. DCSF (2008) offers very helpful guidance on information sharing and the issues to consider.

Other relevant general powers include the National Health Service and Community Care Act 1990, where Section 47 requires local authorities with social services departments to carry out an assessment of need where people appear to be in need of community care services. The Care Standards Act 2000 has helped with institutional abuse in terms of setting higher regulatory standards for care. The Disability Discrimination Act 1995 makes it unlawful to discriminate against someone with a disability by treating them less favourably. It covers employment, training, education, housing and anyone who supplies goods, facilities and services to the public. There are also new provisions to protect whistleblowers from adverse effects on their employment in the Public Interest Disclosure Act 1998.

The Safeguarding Vulnerable Groups Act 2006 has provided a new vetting and barring scheme. The Act came as a result of the Soham murders when Bichard (Home Office, 2004) was asked to look into what had gone wrong with recruitment and barring systems to allow Ian Huntley, who had a questionable past, to work in a school and then perpetrate his crimes against two young girls in Soham. The Safeguarding Vulnerable Groups Act 2006 has two functions, both run by a new Independent Safeguarding Authority. The first function is barring unsuitable workers and was implemented in October 2009. The Protection of Vulnerable Adults list is now being run by the Independent Safeguarding Authority and has a widened brief in terms of referral and workers covered by it. The second function is the vetting of new staff to be implemented in November 2010. There has been a media outcry about this new scheme with many myths surrounding it (e.g. Daily Telegraph, 2009). It is currently being reviewed as a consequence. The scheme is a positive vetting scheme and once a worker or volunteer is cleared as suitable to work with vulnerable adults or children their name is added to the new Independent Safeguarding Authority list and this list is regularly updated by new information.

The other big change in adult protection law in recent years has been the implementation of the Sexual Offences Act 2003, which repeals all previous legislation on sexual offences. Consent is a key issue in the Act and the freedom to make choices. The main sexual offences are rape (now including penile penetration of the mouth, anus or vagina), assault by penetration, sexual assault by touching and causing sexual activity without consent. Sexual relations with certain adult relatives have been clarified. There are a set of offences in relation to mentally disordered adults where choice is impeded. This includes adults with mental health problems or learning disability. There is specific protection from the misuse of a position of trust. It is an offence for someone who is in a relationship of care to have a sexual relationship with the mentally disordered adult.

In the area of neglect, there are limited powers. The use of the National Assistance Act 1948, section 47, has been used occasionally in relation to neglect or self-neglect. This allows the removal to suitable premises of people in need of care and attention who are:

suffering from chronic disease or, being aged, infirm or physically incapacitated and living in insanitary conditions and are unable to devote to themselves and are not receiving from other persons, proper care and attention.

This has to be decided by the community physician and is still an option even after the Human Rights Act 1998. The Mental Health Act 1983 makes it an offence to neglect or ill-treat those with mental disorder who are in hospital, nursing homes or subject to guardianship. Also, where a person assumes a duty of care for an infirm person but is indifferent or reckless to obvious risk of injury, he or she may be guilty of manslaughter should that person die (Stone, 1997). The Mental Capacity Act creates a new criminal offence of ill-treatment or neglect of an adult who lacks mental capacity. The Carers (Recognition and Services) Act 1995 and all the provision for assessment and support of carers is of course relevant in reducing the risk of neglect in domestic situations.

In financial abuse, there are various criminal legislation provisions and other protective measures. Many offences constitute theft and need to be dealt with as such. The Fraud Act 2006 has extended the options in prosecuting. The Mental Capacity Act also provides protection through Lasting Powers of Attorney and Deputies with far more safeguards built into these than previously.

In physical abuse, the Family Law Act 1996 protects vulnerable and other adults in domestic violence situations. It provides for the making of Occupation Orders or non-molestation orders against anyone with whom the victim is 'associated', including spouses, cohabitees, co-tenants or relatives. The Crime Victims and Domestic Violence Act 2004 has added a wider range of relationships to this list and has also added a new criminal offence of causing or allowing the death of a vulnerable adult. There are many situations where domestic violence powers could be useful for vulnerable adults. All the criminal legislation in relation to assaults and violent crimes is relevant in working with physically abused vulnerable adults, and civil action can also be taken by an individual. Where a vulnerable adult is being threatened in some way, the Protection from Harassment Act 1997 can be used to gain an order to help the victim.

The limited emphasis on criminal routes to resolving adult abuse is beginning to change slowly. The Youth Justice and Criminal Evidence Act 1999 and the consequent guidance issued by the Home Office (2001) mean that there is far more prospect of vulnerable adults being able to be heard in court. A series of special measures gives many of the same provisions to vulnerable adults that children have had access to for some time. The use of video interviews as admissible evidence will be particularly beneficial for adults who have been abused, and will also make more demands for evidentially sound interviews. The provision in the Act does not only relate to abuse situations but to any witnessing of crimes. This therefore does not assume a role for a social worker. It is unclear yet how much joint working there will be between the police and social workers, with many areas developing separate training and guidance.

Research into the use of special measures would suggest where they are used that witnesses are more satisfied but only 14 per cent of uses are for those with illness or disability and 5 per cent for adults with learning disability (Hamlyn et al., 2004). Burton, Evans and

Sanders (2006) showed the police were finding it difficult to identify vulnerable and intimidated witnesses and there was limited use of video interviews. Special measures were often applied for very late, which defeated the object of putting the mind of the vulnerable adult at ease.

There has been a long-standing campaign led by Action on Elder Abuse for new legislation in the area of safeguarding adults. This was included in the recent *No Secrets* review. There are two aspects to the campaign for legislation, one around strategy or organisation and the other around intervention in individual service users' lives. In terms of individual service users there has been discussion about a duty to act and a duty to co-operate. In the case of Hounslow X and Y 2008 two adults with learning disability were harassed and ill-treated by youths and Hounslow was initially required to pay compensation for failing to protect the couple from significant harm. This was overturned on appeal when the Lords stated that there is no such general duty of protection on the local authority. In the Adult Support and Protection (Scotland) Act 2007 Scotland have introduced new powers in relation to adults at risk with a council's duty to make enquiries and a right to enter premises. There are also powers to assess and to remove in certain situations of risk. It is too early to know how these are working. There appears to be little political interest in a change in legislation in the rest of the UK currently despite many of the responses to the review supporting such a change. The current Law Commission Review may lead to changes in this area.

Future and conclusion

For the worker within the field of community care, it is important to keep safeguarding adults in the context of all other good work with vulnerable adults. Child protection has had to be balanced with an emphasis on refocusing services, and the need in adult protection is to place protective work within a framework of positive attention to the vulnerable adult's welfare. As policies and law develop to protect adults more effectively, it will be necessary to keep this balance. The current emphasis on safeguarding adults is long overdue and needs to be firmly placed within a high standard of work with vulnerable adults to be of benefit to them.

RECOMMENDED READING

Bennett, G., Kingston, P. and Penhale, B. (1997) *The Dimensions of Elder Abuse.* Basingstoke: Macmillan

Department of Health (2000) *No Secrets: Guidance on developing and implementing multi-agency policies and procedures to protect vulnerable adults from abuse.* London: HMSO

Decalmer, P. and Glendenning, F. (1997) *The Mistreatment of Elderly People.* London: Sage

Williams, C. (1995) *Invisible Victims: Crime and Abuse Against People with Learning Disabilities.* London: Jessica Kingsley

References

Abberley, P. (1987) The concept of oppression and the development of a social theory of disability. *Disability, Handicap and Society*, 2 (187): 5–19

Abercrombie, N. (1994) *Penguin Dictionary of Sociology*. London: Penguin

Abrams, P. (1977) Community care. *Policy and Politics*, 6: 125–151

Acheson, D. (1998) *Independent Inquiry into Inequalities in Health*. London: HMSO

Action for Blind People (2008) *Report on Verbal and Physical Abuse towards Blind and Partially sighted people across the UK*. London: Action for Blind People

Action on Elder Abuse (1995) *Everybody's Business: Taking action on elder abuse*. London: Action on Elder Abuse

Action on Elder Abuse (2006) *Adult Protection Data Collection and Reporting Requirements*. London: Action on Elder Abuse

Adams, R. (2002) *Social Policy For Social Work*. Basingstoke: Palgrave

AIMS (2001) *Aims Alerters' Guide – Complete guidance for staff involved in adult protection*. Brighton: Pavilion

Aitken, L. and Griffin, G. (1996) *Gender Issues in Elder Abuse*. London: Sage

Alaszewski, A. and Horlick-Jones, T. (2004) Integrated health and social care for older persons: theoretical and conceptual issues, in K. Leichsenning and A. Alaszewski (eds) *Providing Integrated Health and Social Care for Older Persons: A European overview of issues at stake*. Hampshire: Ashgate, Aldershot, 53–94

Allen, G. (1985) *Family Life*. Oxford: Basil Blackwell

Allen, G. (1990) Social work, community care and 'informal networks', in Davies, M. (ed.) *The Sociology of Social Work*. London: Routledge

Alt, J.E. and Chrystal, K.A. (1983) *Political Economics*. Brighton: Wheatsheaf

Anon (2004) Fears Over 'Right to Die' Debate and Bill. *Community Care*, 14 October 2004 www.communitycare.co.uk/Articles/2004/10/14/46662/fears-over-right-to-die-debate-and-bill.html (accessed 1 February 2010)

Anonymous Family Carer (2008) In Control? Making sure we're not out of control! Some issues for people considering a direct payment or individualised budget. *Journal of Adult Protection*, 10 (3), August 2008

Arber, S. and Gilbert, M. (1989) Men: the forgotten carers. *Sociology*, 23: 111–118

Ashton, G., Letts P., Oates L. and Terrell, M. (2006) *Mental Capacity: The New Law*. Bristol: Jordan Publishing

Association of Directors of Social Services (2005) *Safeguarding Adults – A National Framework of Standards for good practice and outcomes in adult protection work*. www.adass.org.uk/images/stories/Publications/Guidance/safeguarding.pdf

Atkin, K. (1991) Community care in a multi-racial society. *Policy and Politics*, 19: 3

Audit Commission (1986) *Making a Reality of Community Care*. London: PSI

Baker, A.A. (1975) Granny battering. *Modern Geriatrics*, 5 (8): 20–24

Baldock, J. and Ungerson, C. (1991) 'What d'ya want if ya'don't want money', in Mclean, M. and Groves, D. (eds) *Women's Issues in Social Policy*. London: Routledge

Baldwin, S. and Twigg, J. (1991) Women and community care – reflections on a debate, in Maclean, M. and Groves, D. (eds) *Women's Issues in Social Policy*. London: Routledge

Ballinger, B.R., Ballinger, C.B., Reid, A.H. and McQueen, E. (1991) The psychiatric symptoms, diagnoses and care needs of 100 mentally handicapped patients. *British Journal of Psychiatry*, 158: 251–254

Banks, S. (1995a) *Ethics and Values in Social Work*. Hampshire: Macmillan

Banks, S. (1995b) in Skerrett, D. (2000) Social work — A shifting paradigm. *Journal Of Social Work Practice*, 14 (1): 63

Barbera, R. (2008) Relationships and the research process: participatory action research and social work. *Journal of Progressive Human Services*, 19 (2): 140–159

Barnes, C. and Mercer, G. (2006) *Independent Futures: Creating User-Led Disability Services in a Disabling Society*. Bristol: Policy Press

Barnes, C., Mercer, G. and Shakespeare, T. (1999) *Exploring Disability: A Sociological Introduction*. Cambridge: Polity Press

Barritt, A. (1990) *Innovations in Community Care*. London: FPSC

Bartlett, P. (2005) *Blackstone's Guide to the Mental Capacity Act 2005*. Oxford: Oxford University Press

Bartlett, W., Proper, C., Wilson, D. and LeGrand, J. (eds) (1994) *Quasi-markets in the Welfare State*. Bristol: SAUS

Baxter, K., Glendinning, C and Clarke, S. (2008) Making informed choices in social care: the importance of accessible information. *Health and Social Care in the Community*, 16 (2): 197–207

Bayliss, K. (2000) Social work values, anti-discriminatory practice and working with older lesbian service users. *Social Work Education*, 19 (1): 45–53

BBC News (2008) Does disability hate crime exist, 19/8/2008. http://news.bbc.co.uk/1/hi/magazine/7570305.stm

BBC News (2009) Spotlight on disability hate crime, 29/9/2009. http://news.bbc.co.uk/1/hi/uk/8280577.stm

BBC News (2009) Police 'will learn' from deaths, 29/9/2009. http://news.bbc.co.uk/1/hi/england/leicestershire/8281051.stm

BBC News (2010) Man, 64, collapses and dies after 'abuse from youths', 11/3/2010. http://news.bbc.co.uk/1/hi/england/manchester/8561513.stm

BBC News (2010) County Durham torture murderer jailed for life, 12/2/2010. http://news.bbc.co.uk/1/hi/england/8512834.stm

Beeler, J.A., Rawls, T.W., Herdt, G. and Cohler, B.J. (1999) The needs of older lesbians and gay men in Chicago. *Journal of Gay and Lesbian Social Services*, 9 (1): 31−49

Bennett, G. and Kingston, P. (1993) *Elder Abuse: Concepts, Theories and Interventions*. London: Chapman and Hall

Bennett, G., Kingston, P. and Penhale, B. (1997) *The Dimensions of Elder Abuse*. London: Macmillan

Berger, R.M. (1982) The unseen minority: Older gays and lesbians. *Social Work*, 27: 236−242

Berkman, C.S. and Zinberg, G. (1997) Homophobia and heterosexism in social workers. *Social Work*, 42: 319−332

Berlin, I. (1969) *Four Essays on Liberty*. Oxford: Oxford University Press

Better Regulation Commission (2006) *Risk, Responsibility and Regulation – Whose risk is it anyway?* London: Better Regulation Commission

Beveridge, W. (1942) *The Beveridge Report*. London: HMSO

Bewley, C. (1997) *Money Matters – Helping people with learning difficulties have more control over their money*. London: Values into Action

Biggs, S. (1993) User participation and interprofessional collaboration in community care. *Journal of Interprofessional Care*, 7 (2): 151–159

Biggs, S. (1996) A family concern: elder abuse in British social policy. *Critical Social Policy*, 16 (2): 63−88

Biggs, S., Phillipson, C. and Kingston, P. (1995) *Elder Abuse in Perspective*. Buckingham: Open University Press

Binnie, A. and Titchen, A. (1999) *Freedom to Practice: The Development of Patient Centered Nursing*. London: Butterworth Heinemann

Blair, T. (1998) Third Way: New Politics For a New Century. *Fabian Pamphlet* 588. London: The Fabian Society

Blair, T. (2004) Labour Party Conference Speech, 11 October 2004

Bohan, J. (1996) *Psychology and Sexual Orientation: Coming to Terms*. London: Routledge

Boyle, G. (2009) The Mental Capacity Act 2005 Deprivation of Liberty Safeguards and people with dementia: the implications for social care regulation. *Health and Social Care in the Community*, 17 (4): 415−422

Bradshaw, J. (1972) The concept of social need. *New Society*, 30: 640−643

Braye, S. and Preston-Shoot, M. (1995) *Empowering Practice in Social Care*. Buckingham: Open University Press

Brechin, A. (2000) *Critical Practice in Health and Social Care*. London: Sage

Breckman, R. and Adelman, R. (1988) *Strategies for Helping Victims of Elder Mistreatment*. London: Sage

Briere, J., Woo, R., McRae, B., Foltz, J. and Sitzman, R. (1997) Childhood sexual abuse and physical abuse as factors in adult psychiatric illness. *American Journal of Psychiatry*, 144: 1426–1430

Brotman, S., Ryan, B. and Cormier, R. (2003) the health and social service needs of gay and lesbian elders and their families in Canada. *The Gerontologist*, 43 (2): 192–202

Brown, H., Kingston, P. and Wilson, B. (1999) Adult protection: an overview of research and policy. *The Journal of Adult Protection*, 1 (1): 6–16

Brown, H. and Stein, J. (1998) Implementing adult protection policies in Kent and East Sussex. *Journal of Social Policy*, 27 (3), 371–396

Brown, H. and Turk, V. (1992) Defining sexual abuse as it affects adults with learning disabilities. *Mental Handicap*, 20: 44–55

Brown, H. and Turk, V. (1993) *It could never happen here: the prevention and treatment of sexual abuse of adults with learning disabilities in residential settings*. Chesterfield: Association for Residential Care and National Association for the Protection from Sexual Abuse of Adults and Children with Learning Disabilities

Brown, H., Stein, J. and Turk, V. (1995) The sexual abuse of adults with learning disabilities: Report of a second 2 year incidence survey. *Mental Handicap Research*, 8 (1): 3–24

Bulmer, M. (1987) *The Social Basis of Community Care*. Winchester, MA: Allen & Unwin

Burke, B. and Harrison, P. (2002) Anti-oppressive practice, in R. Adams, L. Dominelli, and M. Payne (eds) *Social Work: Themes, Issues and Critical Debates* (2nd edn). London: Palgrave

Burton, M., Evans, R. and Sanders, A. (2006) *Evaluation of the Use of Special Measures*. London: Home Office

Butler, J. (1994) Origins and early development, in Robinson, R. and Le Grand, J. (eds) *Evaluating the NHS Reforms*. Newbury: King's Fund Institute

Cairns, R., Buchanan, A., David, A.S., Hayward, P., Richardson, G. and Szmukler, G. (2005) Prevalence and predictors of mental incapacity in psychiatric inpatients. *British Journal of Psychiatry*, 187: 379–385

Camden and Islington Community Health Services NHS Trust (1999) *Beech House Inquiry Report of the internal inquiry relating to the mistreatment of patients residing at Beech House, St Pancras Hospital during the period March 1993–April 1996*. London: Camden & Islington Community Health Services NHS Trust

CareKnowledge (2008) *'In Control' – a focus on the individual*. CareKnowledge Special Report 15, September 2008. www.careknowledge.com

Care Quality Commission (2007) *Safeguarding Adults Protocol and Guidance*. Newcastle: CSCI.

Care Quality Commission (2010) *The State of Health Care and Adult Social Care in England: Key Themes and Quality of Services in 2009*. HMSO at www.cqc.org.uk

Care Services Improvement Partnership (2006) *Increasing the Uptake of Direct Payments: A self-assessment and action planning guide for local councils with social services responsibilities and their partners*. www.dh.gov.uk

Care Services Improvement Partnership (2007) *Self Directed Support – A Briefing*. www.kc.csip.org.uk

Carr, S. (2008) *Personalisation: a rough guide*, Adult Services Report 20. London: Social Care Institute for Excellence (SCIE)

Carr, S. and Dittrich, R. (2008) *Personalisation: A rough guide*. London: Social Care Institute for Excellence

Carter, G. and Jancar, J. (1983) Mortality in the mentally handicapped: a 50 year survey at the Stoke Park group of hospitals (1930–1980). *Journal of Mental Deficiency Research*, 27: 143–156

Casement, P. (1985) in Bray, S. and Preston-Shoot, M. (1995) *Empowering Practice in Social Care*. Buckingham: Open University Press

CCETSW (1989) *Multi Disciplinary Teamwork, Models of Good Practice*. London: CCETSW

CCETSW (1996) *Equal Opportunities Policy Statement*. London: CCETSW

Central England People First (2000) *Who Are We*. www.peoplefirst.org.uk/whoarewe.html

Chapman, T., Goodwin, S. and Hennelly, R. (1991) A new deal for the mentally ill?, *Critical Social Policy*, 11(32): 5–20

Circles Network (2008) *Person Centred Planning*. www.circlesnetwork.org.uk

Clark, H. and Spafford, J. (2002) Adapting to a culture of user control? *Social Work Education*, 21 (2): 247–257

Clarke, J. (1998) Thriving on chaos, in Carter, J. (ed.) *Post-modernity and the Fragmentation of Welfare*. New York: Routledge

Clarke, J. and Newman, J. (1998) *The Managerial State*. London: Sage

Clarke, J., Gerwitz, S. and McLaughlin, E. (eds) (2000) *New Managerialism, New Welfare?* London: Sage (in association with OU)

Clifford, D. (1991) *The Social Costs and Rewards of Caring*. Aldershot: Brookfield

Clough, R. (1995) *Foreword – Elder abuse and the law*. Paper presented at the First Annual Conference of Action on Elder Abuse, Lancaster University 1994

Cochrane, A. (1998) Globalisation, fragmentation and local welfare citizenship, in Carter, J. (ed.) *Post-modernity and the Fragmentation of the Welfare State*. New York: Routledge

Commission for Social Care Inspection (2004) *Direct Payments: What are the Barriers?* London: Commission for Social Care Inspection

Commission for Social Care Inspection (2006) *Making Choices: Taking Risks – A discussion paper*. London: Commission for Social Care Inspection

Commission for Social Care Inspection (2008) *Social Services Performance Assessment Framework Indicators Adults 2007–08*. www.cqc.org.uk

Commission for Social Care Inspection, Healthcare Commission, Mental Health Act Commission (2009) *Commissioning Services and Support for People with Learning Disabilities and Complex Needs – National Report of Joint Review*. www.cqc.org.uk

Community Care (2007) *Government aims to make direct payments the norm*. 11 December. www.communitycare.co.uk

Community Care (2009) *Expert guide to personalisation*. www.communitycare.co.uk

Conservative Party. *Conservative Party Manifesto*. www.conservativemanifesto.com/1987

Cooke, L. (1997) Cancer and learning disability. *Journal of Intellectual Disability Research*, 41 (4): 312–316

Cooper, C., Selwood, A., Blanchard, M., Walker, Z., Bizard, R. and Livingston, G. (2009) Abuse of people with dementia by family carers: representative cross sectional survey. *British Medical Journal*, 338: b155

Corbett, J. (1989) The quality of life in the independence curriculum disability, in French, S. (1991) What's so great about independence? *The New Beacon*, 75 (886): 153–156

Corbett J. (2007) *Health Care Provision and People with Learning Disabilities: A Guide for Health Professionals*. Chichester: John Wiley and Sons

Corrigan, P. (2005) *Registering Choice: How Primary Care Should Change to Meet Patient Needs*. London: The Social Market Foundation

Creswell, S. (1996) Creative deceptions. *Community Care*, 2 May 1996

Cronin, A. (2006) Sexuality in gerontology: a heteronormative presence, a queer absence, in S.O. Daatland and Simon Biggs (eds) *Ageing and Diversity: Multiple Pathways in Later Life*. London: Sage

Crosland, C.A.R. (1956) *The Future of Socialism*. London: Jonathan Cape

Crosland, C.A.R. (1974) *Socialism Now and Other Essays.* London: Jonathan Cape

Crown Prosecution Service (2009) *Policy for Prosecuting Cases of Disability Hate Crime*. www.cps.gov.uk/publications/prosecution/disability_hate_crime_leaflet.pdf

Crown Prosecution Service (2010) *Freedom of information disclosures*. www.cps.gov.uk/publications/docs/foi_disclosures/2009/disclosure-63.pdf (accessed 1 February 2010)

Daily Telegraph (2009) Criminal records checks are turning us into a nation of suspects. 28 October

Dale, N. (1996) *Working with Families, Children with Special Needs*. London: Routledge

Dalley, G. (1988) *Ideologies of Caring*. Basingstoke: Macmillan Education

Dalrymple, J. and Burke, B. (1996) *Anti Oppressive Practice. Social Care and the Law*. Buckingham: Open University Press

D'Augelli, A.R., Grossman, A.H., Hershberger, S. and O'Connell, T.S. (2001) Aspects of mental health among older lesbian, gay and bisexual adults. *Aging and Mental Health*, 5 (2): 149–158

David, M. (1986) in Levitas R., *The New Right*. Cambridge: Polity Press

Davies, C., Finlay, L. and Bullman, A. (1999) *Changing Practice in Health and Social Care*. London: Sage

Davies, D. (1996) Homophobia and heterosexism, in Davies, D. and Neal, C. (eds) *Pink Therapy: A guide for counsellors and therapists working with lesbian, gay and bisexual clients*. Buckingham: Open University Press

Deacon, S., Minichiello, V. and Plummer, D. (1995) Sexuality and older people: revisiting the assumptions. *Educational Gerontology*, 21: 497–513

Decalmer, P. and Glendenning, F. (1997) *The Mistreatment of Elderly People*. London: Sage

Dean, H. (1996) *Welfare, Law and Citizenship*. Hertfordshire: Harvester Wheatsheaf

Department for Children, Schools and Families (2008) *Information Sharing: Guidance for practitioners and managers*. London: DCSF

Department for Constitutional Affairs (2007) *Mental Capacity Act 2005 Code of Practice*. London: HMSO

Department of Communities and Local Government (2005) *Glossary of Terms – Social Exclusion*. www.neighbourhood.gov.uk/glossary.asp#S

Department of Health (1987) *Promoting Better Health*. London: HMSO

Department of Health (1989) *Caring for People, Community Care in the Next Decade and Beyond* (Cmnd. 849). London: HMSO

Department of Health (1990) *The NHS and Community Care Act*. London: HMSO

Department of Health (1993) *No Longer Afraid, The safeguarding of elderly people in domestic settings: Practice guidelines*. London: HMSO

Department of Health (1997) *The New NHS: Modern, Dependable*. London: HMSO

Department of Health (1998) *Modernising Social Services: Promoting Independence, Improving Protection, Raising Standards*. Cmd. 4169. London: HMSO

Department of Health (1999) *The NHS Plan*. London: HMSO

Department of Health (2000) *No Secrets: Guidance on Developing and Implementing Multi-agency Policies and Procedures to Protect Vulnerable Adults from Abuse*. London: HMSO

Department of Health (2001a) *Valuing People, A new strategy for learning disability for the 21st century*. London: HMSO

Department of Health (2001b) *National Services Framework for Older People*. London: HMSO

Department of Health (2001c) *Valuing People: Improving life chances for people with learning disabilities for the 21st century*. Cmnd. 5086. London: HMSO

Department of Health (2002) *Fair Access to Care Services: Policy Guidance*. London: Department of Health

Department of Health (2005a) *Mental Capacity Act*. London: Department of Health

Department of Health (2005b) *Independence, Well-being and Choice*. London: HMSO

Department of Health (2006a) *Our Health, Our Care, Our Say: A New Direction for Community Services*. Cmnd. 6737. London: HMSO

Department of Health (2006b) *Working Together to Safeguard Children, A guide to inter-agency working to safeguard and promote the welfare of children*. London: HMSO

Department of Health (2007) *Independence, Choice and Risk: A guide to best practice in supported decision making*. London: HMSO

Department of Health (2008) *Putting People First: A shared vision and commitment to the transformation of adult social care*. London: HMSO

Department of Health (2009a) *Reference Guide to Consent for Examination or Treatment* (2nd edn). London: HMSO

Department of Health (2009b) *Valuing People Now: A New Three-Year Strategy for People with Learning Disabilities (Executive Summary)*. www.dh.gov.uk

Department of Health (2009c) *Good Learning Disability Partnership Boards: 'Making it happen for everyone'*. www.dh.gov.uk

Department of Health (2009d) *A Summary of Changes to Direct Payments*. www.dh.gov.uk

Department Of Health (2009e) *The Bradley Report – Lord Bradley's review of people with mental health problems or learning disabilities in the criminal justice system*. www.dh.gov.uk/en/Publicationsandstatistics/Publications/PublicationsPolicyAndGuidance/DH_098694

Department Of Health (2009f) *Valuing Employment Now – Real jobs for people with learning disabilities*. www.dh.gov.uk/en/Publicationsandstatistics/Publications/PublicationsPolicyAndGuidance/DH_101401

Department Of Health (2009g) *Valuing People Now: The Delivery Plan*. London: HMSO

Department Of Health (2010) *Working Together to Safeguard Children, A guide to inter-agency working to safeguard and promote the welfare of children*. London: HMSO

Department of Social Security (1998) *A New Contract For Welfare*. Cmd. 3805. London: HMSO

DHSS (1981) *Growing Older*. London: HMSO

DHSS (1984) *The Enabling Role of Social Service Departments*. London: HMSO

DHSS (1986) Cumberledge Report. *Neighbourhood Nursing*. London: HMSO

DHSS (1989) White Paper: *Caring for People*. London: HMSO

Disability Now (2010) *Online Hate Crime Dossier of Cases 2006 – 7*. www.disabilitynow.org.uk/the-hate-crime-dossier

Disability Rights Commission (2006) *Equal Treatment – Closing the Gap*. Via NHS Evidence. www.library.nhs.uk/learningdisabilities/ViewResource.aspx?resID=187482

Doucette, J. (1986) *Violent Acts Against Disabled Women*. Toronto: Disabled Women's Network (DAWN)

Dow, J. (2004) Direct payments. *Journal of Integrated Care*, 12 (2): 20 – 23

Duffy, S. (2003) *Keys to Citizenship: A guide to getting good support for people with learning disabilities*. Birkenhead: Paradigm Consultancy and Development Agency

Duffy, S. (2004) *Person Centred Approaches: Next Steps Workbook on Person Centred Care Management*. Birkenhead: Paradigm Consultancy and Development Agency

Dunn (1985) in Thompson, N. (2000, p17) *Theory and Practice: Thinking and Doing in Human Services*. Buckingham: Open University Press

Dyslexia Institute (2005) *The Incidence of Hidden Disabilities in the Prison Population: Yorkshire and Humberside Research*. Egham: The Dyslexia Institute

Eastman, M. (1984) *Old Age Abuse*. Mitcham: Age Concern

Edgerton, R. (1975) Issues relating to the quality of life among mentally retarded persons, in Begab, M. and Richardson, S. (eds) *The Mentally Retarded Person In Society: A Social Science Perspective*. Baltimore: University Park Press

Edwards, J. (2005) Invisibility, safety and psycho-social distress among same-sex attracted women in rural South Australia. *Rural and Remote Health 5* (online), 2005: 343. Available at: www.rrh.org.au

Emerson, E. (2001) *Challenging Behaviour: Analysis and Intervention in People with Severe Intellectual Disabilities*. Cambridge: Cambridge University Press

Emerson, E., Malam, B., Davies, I. and Spencer, K. (2005) *A Survey of Adults With Learning Difficulties in England 2003–4. National Statistics and NHS Health and Social Care* (accessed via DoH at www.dh.gov.uk/prod_consum_dh/groups/dh_digitalassets/@dh/@en/documents/digitalasset/dh_4119944.pdf)

Enfield, S.L. and Tonge, B.J. (1996) Population prevalence of psychopathology in children and adolescents with intellectual disability: II. Epidemiological findings. *Journal of Intellectual Disability Research*, 40: 99–109

Equal Opportunities Commission (1982) *Caring for the Elderly and Handicapped*. Manchester: EOC

Evandrou, M. (1990) *Challenging the Invisibility of Carers*. London: LSE

Fenge, L. (2001) Empowerment and community care – projecting the 'voice' of older people. *Journal of Social and Family Welfare Law*, 23 (4): 427–439

Fenge, L. (2010) Striving for inclusive research: An example of participatory action research with older lesbians and gay men. *British Journal of Social Work*, 40: 878–894

Fenge, L. and Fannin, A. (2009) Sexuality and bereavement: implications for practice with older lesbians and gay men. *Practice: Social Work in Action*

Fennell, G. et al. (1988) in Thompson, N. (1993, p17) *Anti-Discriminatory Practice*. Basingstoke: Macmillan

Finch, A. (1984) Community care: developing non-sexist alternatives, *Critical Social Policy*, 16: 6–18

Finch, J. (1989) *Family Obligation and Social Change*. London: Polity Press

Finch, J. and Groves, D. (1980) Community care and the family. *Journal of Social Policy*, 9 (4): 494

Finkelhor, D. and Pillemer, K.A. (1988) Elder abuse: its relationship to other forms of domestic violence, in Hotaling, G.T., Finkelhor, D., Kirkpatrick, J.T. and Straus, M.A. (eds) *Family Abuse and its Consequences: New Directions in Research*. London: Sage

Finkelstein, V. (2004) Representing disability, Chapter 2 in Swain, J., French, S., Barnes, C. and Thomas, C. (eds) *Disabling Barriers, Enabling Environments* (2nd edn). London: Sage

Finnister, G. (1991) Care in the community: the social security issues. *Social Work and Social Welfare*, Y1: Bl13

Flynn, N. (1989) The New Right and social policy. *Policy and Politics*,17 (2): 97–109

Fokkemer, T. and Kuyper, L. (2009) The relation between social embeddedness and loneliness among older lesbian, gay and bisexual adults in the Netherlands. *Archives of Sexual Behaviour*, 38: 264–275

Foster, M., Harris, J., Jackson, K., Morgan, H. and Glendinning, C. (2006) Personalised social care for adults with disabilities: a problematic concept for front line practice. *Health and Social Care in the Community*, 14 (2): 125–135

Foster, P. (1991) Residential care of frail elderly people: a positive re-assessment. *Social Policy and Administration*, 25: 2

Foundation for People with Learning Disabilities (2007) *Statistics about people with learning disabilities*. www.learningdisabilities.org.uk/information/learning-disabilities-statistics/#many

Freire, P. (1972) *Pedagogy of the Oppressed*. Harmondsworth: Penguin

Fullmer, E., Shenk, D. and Eastland, L. (1999) Negating identity: a feminist analysis of the social invisibility of older lesbians. *Journal of Women and Aging*, 11 (2-3): 131–148

Fyson, R. (2009) Independence and learning disabilities: why we must also recognise vulnerability. *Journal of Integrated Care*, 17 (1): 3–8

Gates, B. (ed.) (2007) *Learning Disabilities: Towards Inclusion* (5th edn). Edinburgh: Churchill Livingstone/Elsevier

Gates, B. and Barr, O. (2009) *Oxford Handbook of Learning and Intellectual Disability Nursing*. Oxford: Oxford University Press

Gay and Grey in Dorset (2006) *Lifting the Lid on Sexuality and Ageing*. Dorset: Help and Care Development

Geelen, R. and Soons, P. (1996) Rehabilitation and 'everyday' motivation model. *Patient Education and Counselling* (1996) pp69–77

George, V. and Wilding, P. (1985) *Ideology and Social Welfare* (2nd edn). Boston: RKP

George, V. and Wilding, P. (1994) *Welfare and Ideology*. Hertfordshire: Harvester Wheatsheaf

Gibbs, J., Evans, M. and Rodway, S. (1987) *Report of the Inquiry into Nye Bevan Lodge*. London: Borough of Southwark

Gilbert, L.M., Williams, R.L. and McLaughlin, T.F. (1986) Use of assisted reading to increase correct reading rates and decrease error rates of students with learning disabilities. *Journal of Applied Behavior Analysis*, 29: 255–257

Gilbert, N. (1983) *Capitalism and the Welfare State*. New Haven: Yale University Press

Glasby, J. and Littlechild, R. (2002) *Social Work and Direct Payments*. Bristol: Policy Press

Glendinning, C. (1990) Dependency and interdependency, the incomes of informal carers and the impact of social security. *Journal of Social Policy*, 19: 4

Glendinning, C. and Baldwin, S. (1988) in Walker, R. and Parker, G. (eds) *Money Matters*. London: Sage

Glendinning, C., Challis, D., Fernandez, J-L., Jacobs, S., Jones, K., Knapp, M., Manthorpe, J., Moran, N., Netten, A., Stevens, M. and Wilberforce, M. (2008) *Evaluation of the Individual Budgets Pilot Programme: Summary Report*. SPRU, PSSRU, Social Care Workforce Research Unit

Glennerster, H., Falkingham, J. and Evandrou, M. (1990) How much do we care? *Social Policy and Administration*, 24(2) 93–103

Glennerster, H., Matsaganis, M., Owens, P. and Hancock, S. (1994) GP fund holding: wild card or winning hand? in Robinson, R. and Le Grand, J. (eds) *Evaluating the NHS Reforms*. Newbury: King's Fund Institute

Goodwin, S. (1989) Community care for the mentally ill in England and Wales. *Journal of Social Policy*, 18(01): 27–52

Gorman, H. (2000) Winning hearts and minds? – Emotional labour and learning for care management work. *Journal of Social Work Practice*, 14 (2): 149–158

Green, N. (1996) in Secker, J., Hill, R., Villeneau, L. and Parkman, S. (2003, p382) Promoting independence: but promoting what and how? *Ageing and Society*, 23: 375–391

Haddon, C. (2004) *The Curious Incident of the Dog in the Night-Time*. New York: Vintage USA

Hadley, R. and Hatch, S. (1981) *Social Welfare and the Failure of the State*. London: George & Unwin

Hall, J. and Newman, S. (2008) *Personalisation and Self Directed Support*. CareKnowledge Special Report 6, April 2008. www.careknowledge.com

Hamlyn, B., Phelps, A. and Sattar, G. (2004) *Survey of Vulnerable and Intimidated Witnesses*. London: Home Office

Hard, S. and Plumb, W. (1987) Sexual abuse of persons with developmental disabilities, in Turk, V. and Brown, H. (1993) The sexual abuse of adults with learning disabilities: results of a two year incidence survey. *Mental Handicap Research*, 6: 193–216

Harris, J. (2000) *Choice and Empowerment for People with a Learning Disability*. British Institute of Learning Disabilities

Harrison, S. and Pollitt, C. (1994) *Controlling Health Professionals*. Buckingham: Open University Press

Hartley, D. (2008) Education, markets and the pedagogy of personalization. *British Journal of Educational Studies*, 56 (4): 365–381

Hayek, F.A. (1960) **The Constitution of Liberty.** Chicago: University of Chicago Press

Hays, T., Fortunato, V. and Minichiello, V. (1997) Insights into the lives of older gay men: a qualitative study with implications for practitioners. *Venereology*, 10 (2): 115–120

Healthcare Commission (2006) *Joint Investigation into the Provision of Services for People with Learning Disabilities at Cornwall Partnership NHS Trust*, available at www.cqc.org.uk/_db/_documents/cornwall_investigation_report.pdf

Healthcare Commission (2007a) *Investigation into the Service for People With Learning Disabilities*. Provided by Sutton and Merton Primary Care Trust January 2007. www.cqc.org.uk/_db/_documents/Sutton_and_Merton_inv_Main_Tag.pdf

Healthcare Commission (2007b) *A Life Like No Other: A National Audit of Specialist Inpatient Healthcare services for People with Learning Difficulties in England*. http://2007ratings.healthcarecommission.org.uk/_db/_documents/LD_audit_report.pdf

Health Service and Local Government Ombudsman (2009) *Six lives: the provision of public services to people with learning disabilities*. www.lg.org.uk/news/2009/mar/ombudsmen-call-review-care-people-learning-disabilities/

Heaphy, B. (2009) Choice and its limits in older lesbian and gay narratives of relational life. *Journal of GLBT Family Studies*, 5 (1/2): 119–138

Heaphy, B., Yip, A. and Thompson, D. (2003) *Lesbian, Gay and Bisexual Lives Over 50*. Nottingham Trent University: York House Publications

Henwood, M. (2008) In control evaluation: users' quality of life improves. *Community Care*, Thursday 8 May 2008. www.communitycare.co.uk

Herring, R. and Thom, B. (1997) The right to take risks: alcohol and older people. *Social Policy and Administration*, 31 (3): 233–246

Higgins, K. (2006) Some victims less equal than others. *Scottish Legal Action Group Journal*, August 2006: 162–163

Hill, M. (ed.) (1991) *Social Work and the European Community*. London: Jessica Kingsley

Hills, J. (1997) *The Future of Welfare*. York: Joseph Rowntree Foundation

Hindess, B. (1987) *Freedom, Equality and the Market*. London: Tavistock Publications

Holland, S. (1980) *The Socialist Challenge*. London: Quartet Books

Hollins, S, Attard, M.T., von Fraunhofer, N. and Sedgwick, P. (1998) Mortality in people with learning disability: risks, causes, and death certification findings in London. *Developmental Medicine and Child Neurology*, 40: 50–56

Home Office (2000) *Setting the Boundaries*. London: Home Office Communication Directorate

Home Office (2001) *Achieving Best Evidence in Criminal Proceedings: Guidance for vulnerable or intimidated witnesses including children*. London: Home Office Communication Directorate

Home Office (2004) *The Bichard Inquiry Report*. London: HMSO

Home Office and Inclusion North (2008) *Learning Disability Hate Crime: Good Practice Guidance for Crime and Disorder Reduction*. www.inclusionnorth.org/documents/Hate%20Crime%20Good%20 Practice%20Guide.pdf

Homer, A.C. and Gilleard, C. (1990) Abuse of elderly people by their carers. *British Medical Journal*, 301: 1359–1362

Hopson, B. (1981) in Herbert, M. (1986, p154) *Psychology for Social Workers*. Basingstoke: Macmillan

House of Commons (2008) House of Lords and House of Commons Joint Committee on Human Rights, *A Life Like Any Other? Human Rights of Adults with Learning Disabilities*. www.publications.parliament. uk/pa/jt200708/jtselect/jtrights/40/40i.pdf

Hudson, B. (1989) Impact of the New Right. *The Health Service Journal*, 99: 1546–7

Hudson, B. (1991) A question of teamwork. *Health Service Journal*, 101: 18–19

Hudson, B. and Ricketts, W. (1980) A strategy for the measurement of homophobia. *Journal of Homosexuality*, 5: 357–372

Hughes, G. (1998) A suitable case for treatments? Constructions of disability, in Saraga, E. (ed.) *Embodying The Social: Constructions of Difference*. London: Routledge

Hugman, R. (1994) Social work and case management in the UK: models of professionalism and elderly people. *Ageing and Society*, 14 (2): 237–253

In Control (2008) *A Report on In Control's Second Phase: Evaluation and Learning 2005–2007.* In Control Publications

In Control (2009) *Research Data for 2008.* www.in-control.org.uk

Independent Living Fund (2009) *User Profile Analysis at 30 September 2009.* www.ilf.org.uk

Independent Online (2009) Action on disability hate crimes, 9/12/2009. www.independent.co.uk/news/uk/home-news/action-on-disability-hate-crimes-1833139.html

Jack, R. (1994) Dependence, power and violation: Gender issues in abuse of elderly people by formal carers, in M. Eastman (ed.) *Old Age Abuse: A new perspective.* London: Chapman Hall

Jack, R. (1998) Institutions in community care, in Jack, R (ed.) *Residential v. Community Care.* Basingstoke: Macmillan

Jacobs, R.J., Rasmussen, L.A. and Hohman, M. (1999) The social support needs of older lesbians, gay men, and bisexuals. *Journal of Gay and Lesbian Social Services,* 1: 1–30

Jamieson, A. and Illsley, R. (1991) *Contrasting European Policies for the Care of Older People.* Aldershot: Avebury Gower Publishing

Jeary, K. (2004) The victims' voice – how is it heard? *Journal of Adult Protection,* 6 (1)

Johnson, M. (1990) The mixed economy of welfare, in Ware, A. and Goodin, R.E. *Needs and Welfare.* London: Sage

Johnson, N. (1990) *Reconstructing the Welfare State.* Hertfordshire: Simon and Schuster

Johnson, N. (1995) Domestic violence: an overview, in Kingston, P. and Penhale, B. (eds) *Family Violence and the Caring Professions.* Basingstoke: Macmillan

Jones, K. (1989) *Experience in Mental Health.* London: Sage

Jones, K. (1998) 'We need the bed' – continuing care and community care, in Jack, R (ed.) *Residential v. Community Care.* Basingstoke: Macmillan

Jones, R. (2005) *Mental Capacity Act Manual.* London: Thomson/Sweet & Maxwell

Jordan, B. (1998) *The New Politics of Welfare.* London: Sage

Jordan, B. (2000) *Social Work and the Third Way, Tough Love as Social Policy.* London: Sage

Jordan, B. (2001) Tough love: Social work, social exclusion and the Third Way. *British Journal of Social Work,* 31(4): 527–546

Joseph Rowntree Foundation (1999) *People with Learning Disabilities and Their Access to Direct Payments Schemes.* www.jrf.org.uk

Kappeler, S. (1995) *The Will to Violence: The Politics of Personal Behaviour.* Cambridge: Polity Press

Kemshall, H. (2002) *Risk, Social Policy and Welfare.* Buckingham: Open University Press

Keynes, J.M. (1936) *The General Theory of Employment, Interest and Money.* London: Macmillan

Killin, D. (1993) Independent living, personal assistance, disabled lesbians and gay men, in C. Barnes (ed.) *Making Our Own Choices: Independent living, personal assistance and disabled people.* Belper: BCODP

King's Fund (2002) *Rehabilitation and Intermediate Care: Policy Documents.* London: King's Fund

Kirby, J. (2000) in Wade, S. and Lees, L. (2002) The who, why, what of intermediate care. *Journal of Community Nursing*, 16: 6–10

Kraan, R.J., Baldock, J., Davies, B., Evers, A., Johansson, L., Knapen, M., Thorslund, M. and Tunissen, C. (1991) *Care for the Elderly: Significant Innovations in Three European Countries*. Boulder: Westview

Ladyman, S. (2004) Vision validated. *Community Care*, 7–13: 44

Langan, M. (1990) Community care in the 90s: the community care White Paper Caring for People. *Critical Social Policy*, 29: 58–70.

Langley, J. (1997) *Meeting the Needs of Older Lesbians and Gay Men*. University of Brighton: Health and Social Policy Research Centre

Langley, J. (2001) Developing anti-oppressive practice empowering social work practice with older lesbian women and gay men. *British Journal of Social Work*, 31: 917–932

Land, H. (1989) in Bulmer, M. *The Goals of Social Policy*. London: Unwin

Lau, E. and Kosberg, J.I. (1979) Abuse of the elderly by informal care providers. *Ageing*, September/October: 11–15

Leadbeater, C. and Miller, P. (2004) *The Pro-Am Revolution: How enthusiasts are changing our economy and society*. London: Demos

Leadbeater, C., Bartlett, J. and Gallagher, N. (2008) *Making it Personal*. London: Demos

Leaper, R. (1971) *Community Work*. National Council of Social Services

Lee, J.A.B. (2000) *The Empowerment Approach to Social Work Practice: Building the Beloved Community*. New York: Columbia Social Work Press

Le Grand, J. and Estrin, S. (1990) *Market Socialism*. Oxford: Clarendon Press

Levitas, R. (1986) *The Ideology of the New Right*. Cambridge: Polity Press

Lewis, J. and Glennerster, H. (1996) *Implementing the New Community Care*. Buckingham: Open University Press

Lewis, J. and Meredith, B. (1988) *Daughters Who Care*. London: Routledge

Licht, S. (1968) *Rehabilitation Medicine*. Baltimore: Waverly Press

Lipshitz, D.S., Kaplan, M.L., Sorkenn, J.B., Faedda, G.L., Chorney, P. and Asnis, G. (1996) Prevalence and characteristics of physical and sexual abuse among psychiatric outpatients. *Psychiatric Services*, 47: 189–191

Liss, P. (1998) Assessing health care need: the conceptual foundation, in Baldwin, S. (ed.) *Needs Assessment and Community Care*. London: Butterworth Heinemann

Lister, R. (1998) In from the margins: citizenship, inclusion and exclusion, in M. Barry and C. Hallett (eds) *Social Exclusion and Social Work*. Lyme Regis: Russell House Publishing

Llewellyn, G. and McConnell, D. (2010) You have to prove yourself all of the time: people with learning disability as parents, Chapter 23 in Grant, G., Ramcharan, R., Flynn, M. and Richardson, M. (eds) *Learning Disability: A Lifecycle Approach* (2nd edn). Maidenhead: OU Press/McGraw-Hill Education

London Borough of Richmond upon Thames (2010) Your support, your way. *The story so far of self-directed support in the London Borough of Richmond upon Thames*. www.in-control.org.uk

Loney, M. (1986) *The Politics of Greed*. London: Pluto Press

Longacre Inquiry (1998) *Independent Longacre Inquiry*. Buckinghamshire: Buckinghamshire County Council

Lord Chancellor's Department (1997) *Who Decides? Making Decisions on Behalf of Mentally Incapacitated Adults*. London: HMSO

Lord Chancellor's Department (1999) *Making Decisions, The government's proposals for making decisions on behalf of mentally incapacitated adults*. London: HMSO

Luengo-Fernandez, R., Leal, J. and Gray, A. (2010) *Dementia 2010 The economic burden of dementia and associated research funding in the United Kingdom*. Health Economics Research Centre/Alzheimer's Research Trust

Lymbery, M. (2005) *Social Work with Older People: Context Policy and Practice*. London: Sage

McCarthy, M. (1989) *The Politics of Welfare*. London: Macmillan

McClimens, A. and Combes, H. (2010) (Almost) Everything you wanted to know about sexuality and learning disability but were too afraid to ask, Chapter 18 in Grant, G., Ramcharan, R., Flynn, M. and Richardson, M. (eds) 2010 *Learning Disability: A Lifecycle Approach* (2nd edn). Maidenhead: OU Press/McGraw-Hill Education

McConkey, R. (2007) Leisure and work, Chapter 10 in Gates, B. (ed.) *Learning Disabilities: Towards Inclusion* (5th edn). Edinburgh: Churchill Livingstone/Elsevier

McCreadie, C. (2001) *Making Connections: Good practice in the prevention and management of elder abuse*. London: Kings College

McDonald, A. (1999) *Understanding Community Care: A guide for social workers*. Hampshire: Macmillan

McKenzie, F. and McAlister, H. (2010) The roots of bio-medical diagnosis, Chapter 3 in Grant, G., Ramcharan, R., Flynn, M. and Richardson, M. (eds) *Learning Disability: A Lifecycle Approach* (2nd edn). Maidenhead: OU Press/McGraw-Hill Education

Mandelstam, M. (2009) *Community Care Practice and the Law* (4th edn). London: Jessica Kingsley

Mangen, S. (1985) *Mental Health Care in the European Community*. London: Croom Helm

Manthorpe, J. (2008) Rural areas and personalization. *Community Care*, 1744: 34–36

Manthorpe, J., Penhale, B. and Stanley, N. (eds) (1999) *Institutional Abuse Perspectives Across the Life Course*. London: Routledge

Manthorpe, J., Jacobs, S., Rapaport, J., Challis, D., Netten, A., Glendinning, C., Stevens, Wilberforce, M., Knapp, M. and Harris, J. (2008) Training for change: Early days of individual budgets and the implications for social work and care management practice: A qualitative study of the views of trainers. *British Journal of Social Work*, 39(7): 1291–1305

Maria Colwell Inquiry Report (1974) *Committee of Inquiry into the Death of Maria Colwell*. East Sussex Social Services

Martin, J.I. and Knox, J. (2000) Methodological and ethical issues in research on lesbians and gay men. *Social Work Research*, 24 (1): 51–59

Mayo, M. (1994) *Communities and Caring. The Mixed Economy of Welfare*. Basingstoke: Macmillan

Means, R. and Smith, R. (1998) *Community Care: Policy and Practice* (2nd edn). Basingstoke: Macmillan

Mencap (2000) *Living in Fear*. London: Mencap

Mencap (2004) *Treat Me Right*. www.mencap.org.uk/document.asp?id=316

Mencap (2007) *Death by Indifference*. www.mencap.org.uk/document.asp?id=284

Mencap (2009) *Bullying, Harassment and Hate Crime Factsheet*. www.mencap.org.uk/document.asp?id=12734

Mencap (2010) *Hate Crime, Real Life Stories*. www.mencap.org.uk/page.asp?id=1954

Messman-Moore, T.L. and Long, P.J. (2000) Child sexual abuse and revictimisation I: the form of adult sexual abuse, adult physical abuse and adult psychological maltreatment. *Journal of Interpersonal Violence*, 15 (5): 489–502

Michael, K. (Chair) (2008) *Independent Inquiry into Access to Healthcare for People with Learning Disabilities – 'Healthcare for All'*. www.dh.gov.uk/en/Publicationsandstatistics/Publications/PublicationsPolicyAndGuidance/DH_099255

Middleton, L. (1994) in Nolan, M. and Caldock, K. (1996, p80) Assessment: Identifying the barriers to good practice. *Health and Social Care in the Community*, 4 (2): 77–79

Milner, J. (2001) *Women and Social Work: Narrative Approaches*. Basingstoke: Palgrave

Milner, J. and O'Byrne, P. (1998) *Assessment in Social Work*. London: Palgrave

Milner, J. and O'Byrne, P. (2002) *Assessment in Social Work* (2nd edn). Basingstoke: Palgrave

Mind (2007) *Another assault, Mind's campaign for equal access to justice for people for people with mental health problems*. London: Mind

Minichiello, V. (2000) in Secker, J. et al. (2003, p253) Promoting independence: but promoting what and how? *Ageing and Society*, 23, 2003: 375–391

Ministry of Justice (2008) *Mental Capacity Act 2005 Deprivation of Liberty Safeguards Code of Practice to supplement the main Mental Capacity Act 2005 Code of Practice*. London: HMSO

Minois, G. (1989) *History of Old Age, from Antiquity to the Renaissance*. Chicago: University of Chicago Press

Mishra, R. (1984) *The Welfare State in Crisis*. New York: St Martins Press

Mitchell, W. and Glendinning, C. (2008) Risk and adult social care: Identification, management and new policies. What does UK research evidence tell us? *Health, Risk and Society*, 10 (3): 297–315

Monk, J. (2006) Do direct payments offer people with learning disabilities greater choice and control?, in Brown, K. (ed.) (2006) *Vulnerable Adults and Community Care*, 56–68. Exeter: Learning Matters

Morgan, O. (1998) *Who Cares? The Great British Health Debate*. Abingdon: Radcliffe Medical Press

Munday, B. (1989) *The Crisis in Welfare*. London: Harvester Wheatsheaf

Murray, J. and Adam, B. (2001) Aging, sexuality and HIV issues among older gay men. *Canadian Journal of Human Sexuality*, 10 (3-4): 75–90

Musingarimi, P. (2008) *Older Gay, Lesbian and Bisexual People in the UK. A Policy Brief*. London: International Longevity Centre – UK (ILCUK). Available at: www.ilcuk.org.uk

National Health Service Information Centre (2010) *Quarterly Analysis of Mental Capacity Act 2005 Deprivation of Liberty Safeguards (DoLS) assessments (England)*. www.ic.nhs.uk/pubs/mentalcapcity09101-3 (accessed 24 March 2010)

National Patient Safety Agency (2003–2005) *Sexual incidents on mental health wards*. London: NPSA

Naylor, L. (2006) Adult protection for community care/vulnerable adults, Chapter 10 in Brown, K. (ed.) 2006 *Vulnerable Adults and Community Care*. Exeter: Learning Matters

Needham, C. (2009) *Co-production: An emerging evidence base for adult social care transformation*. London: SCIE

Nelson, G. and Prilleltensky, I. (2005) *Community Psychology – In Pursuit of Liberation and Well-being*. Hampshire: Palgrave Macmillan

Netten, A., Jones, K., Knapp, M., Fernandez, J., Challis, D., Jacobs, S., Manthorpe, J., Harris, J., Stevens, M., Glendinning, C., Moran, N., Rabiee, P., and Wilberforce, M. (2007) *Individual Budgets Evaluation: A Summary of Early Findings*. IBSEN Network

Nettleton, S. and Burrows, R. (1998) Individualisation processes and social policy, in Carter, J. (ed.) *Post-modernity and the Fragmentation of Welfare*. New York: Routledge

Newman, J., Glendinning, C. and Hughes, M. (2008) Beyond modernisation? Social care and the transformation of welfare governance. *Journal of Social Policy*, 37 (4): 531–557

NHS Scottish Executive (2004) *People With Learning Disability in Scotland: The Health Needs Assessment Report*. Glasgow: NHS Health Scotland

Nibert, D., Cooper, S. and Crossmaker, M. (1989) Assaults against residents of a psychiatric institution: Residents' history of abuse. *Journal of Interpersonal Violence*, 4 (3): 342–349

Nicholas, E. (2003) An outcomes focus on carer assessment and review: value and challenge. *British Journal of Social Work*, 1: 31–47

Nolan, C. (1999) *Under the Eye of the Clock: a Memoir*. London: Phoenix

Nolan, M. (1997) Health and social care, what the future holds for nursing. Keynote address of Nursing Older Persons European Conference at Harrogate

Nolan, M. (2000) in Hancock, S. (2003) *Nursing Standard,* 17 (48): 45–51

Nolan, M., Davies, S. and Grant, G. (2001) *Working with Older People and their Families: Key Issues in Policy and Practice*. Buckingham: Open University Press

Northfield, J. (2010) 'What is Learning Disability – A note On Terminology' on NHS Evidence – learning disabilities. www.library.nhs.uk/learningdisabilities/ViewResource.aspx?resID=154854&tabID=290&catID=6095

Nzira, V. and Williams, P. (2009) *Anti Oppressive Practice in Health and Social Care*. London: Sage

Office of the Deputy Prime Minister (2006) *A Sure Start to Later Life: Ending Inequalities for Older People: A Social Exclusion Unit Final Report*. London: HMSO

Ogg, J. and Bennett, G.C.J. (1992) Elder abuse in Britain. *British Medical Journal*, 305: 998–999

O'Keefe, M., Hills, A., Doyle, M., McCreadie, C., Scholes, S., Constantine, R., Tinker, A., Manthorpe, J., Biggs, S. and Erens, B. (2007) *UK Study of Abuse and Neglect of Older People – Prevalence Study Report*, London: DoH

Oliver, M. (1990) *The Politics Of Disablement*. Basingstoke: Macmillan

Oliver, M. and Sapey, B. (2006) *Social Work with Disabled People* (3rd edn). Basingstoke: Palgrave Macmillan

OPSI (2006) Safeguarding Vulnerable Groups Act 2006. www.opsi.gov.uk/acts/acts2006/pdf/ukpga_20060047_en.pdf

Parker, G. (1985, 1990) *With Due Care and Attention*. London: FPSC

Parker, R. and Aggleton, P. (2003) HIV and AIDS-related stigma and discrimination: a conceptual framework and implications for action. *Social Science and Medicine*, 57: 13–24

Pascal, G. (1986) *Social Policy*. London: Allen and Unwin

Patel, P., Goldberg, D. and Moss, S. (1993) Psychiatric morbidity in older people with moderate and severe learning disability. II: The prevalence study. *British Journal of Psychiatry*, 163: 481–491

Paterson, B. (2001) Myth of empowerment in chronic illness. *Journal of Advance Nursing*, 34 (5); 574–581

Paton, C. (1994) Planning and markets in the NHS, in Bartlett, W. et al. (eds) *Quasi-markets in the Welfare State*. Bristol: SAUS

Pearson, C. (2000) Money talks? Competing discourses in the implementation of direct payments. *Critical Social Policy*, 20 (4)

Pease, B. (2002) Rethinking empowerment: a postmodern reappraisal for emancipatory practice. *British Journal of Social Work*, 32: 135–147

Perring, C. (1989) *Families Caring for People Diagnosed as Mentally Ill*. London: HMSO

Phillips, J. (1996) in Parton, N. (ed.) *Social Theory, Social Work and Social Change*. London: Routledge

Phillipson, C. (1989) in Thompson, N. (1993, p205) *Anti-Discriminatory Practice*. Basingstoke: Macmillan

Pillemer, K.A. and Moore, D.W. (1989) Abuse of patients in nursing homes: findings from a survey of staff. *The Gerontologist*, 29 (3): 314–320

Pillemer, K.A. and Moore, D.W. (1990) Highlights from a study of abuse in nursing homes. *Journal of Elder Abuse and Neglect*, 2 (1/2): 5–29

Pitt, V. (2009) Personalisation: 'Vulnerable will not have to manage budgets'. *Community Care*, 23/10/2009

Pitts, J., Soave, V. and Waters, J. (2009) *Doing It Your Way: The Story of Self Directed Support in Worcestershire*. Worcestershire County Council/In Control Partnerships

Plant, R. (1984) *Equality, Markets and the State.* Fabian Society Pamphlet no. 494

Pollner, M. and Rosenfeld, D. (2000) The cross-culturing work of gay and lesbian elderly. *Advances in Life Course Research,* 5: 99–117

Postle, K. (2002) Working 'between the idea and the reality': ambiguities and tensions in care managers' work. *British Journal of Social Work,* 32: 335–351

Powell, M. and Hewitt, M. (2002) Welfare state and welfare change. *Journal of Social Policy,* 32: 628–629

Priest, H. and Gibbs, M. (2004) *Mental Health Care for People with Learning Disabilities.* Edinburgh: Churchill Livingstone

Priestley, M. (1999) *Disability Politics and Community Care.* London: Jessica Kingsley

Prison Reform Trust (2007) (report author Loucks, N.) *No One Knows: Offenders with learning difficulties and learning disabilities – review of prevalence and associated needs.* www. prisonreformtrust.org.uk/temp/Prevalencecmspfullspreport.pdf

Pritchard, J. (1990) Old and abused. *Social Work Today,* 15 February: 22

Pritchard, J. (1992) *The Abuse of Elderly People: A Handbook for Professionals.* London: Jessica Kingsley

Pritchard, J. (1993) Gang warfare. *Community Care,* 8, July: 22–23

Pritchard, J. (1995) *The Abuse of Older People.* London: Jessica Kingsley

Pritchard, J. (1996) *Working with Elder Abuse.* London: Jessica Kingsley

Pritchard, J. (1999) *Elder Abuse Work, Best practice in Britain and Canada.* London: Jessica Kingsley

Pritchard, J. (2001) *Male Victims of Elder Abuse, Their Experiences and Needs.* London: Jessica Kingsley

Puri, B.K., Lekh, S.K., Langa, A., Zaman, R. and Singh, I. (1995) Mortality in a hospitalized mentally handicapped population: a 10-year survey. *Journal of Intellectual Disability Research,* 39: 442–446.

Quam, J.K. (1993) *Gay and Lesbian Aging.* Children, Youth and family consortium SIECUS Report June/July

Quareshi, H. and Walker A. (1989) *The Caring Relationship.* Basingstoke: Macmillan

Raghaven, R. and Patel, P. (2005) *Learning Disabilities and Mental Health: A Nursing Perspective.* Oxford: Blackwell

Ramon, S. (1991) (ed.) *Beyond Community Care.* Basingstoke: Macmillan Education

Raymont, V., Bingley, W., Buchanan, A., David, A.S. Hayward P., Wessely, S., et al. (2004) Prevalence of mental incapacity in medical inpatients and associated risk factors: cross-sectional study. *The Lancet,* 364: 1421–1427

Redding, D. (1991) Exploding the myth. *Community Care,* 12.12.91

Redfern, S.J. (1998) Long-term care: Is there still a role for nursing? in Jack, R. (ed.) *Residential v. Community Care.* Basingstoke: Macmillan

Richards, S. (2000) Bridging the divide: elders and the assessment process. *British Journal of Social Work,* 30: 37–49

Ricupero, R. (1998) Through a glass darkly. *The World Today*, 54 (11): 277–278

Robbins, D. (1990) Voluntary organisations in the European Community. *Voluntas*,1 (2): 103

Robinson, R. and Le Grand, J. (eds) (1994) *Evaluating the NHS Reforms*. Newbury: King's Fund Institute

Rogers, A. (1997) Vulnerability, health and health care. *Journal Of Advanced Nursing*, 26: 65–72.

Rojek, C. (1988) *Social Work and Received Ideas*. London: Routledge

Ryan, J. and Thomas, F. (1987) *The Politics of Mental Handicap*. London: Free Association Books

Samuel, M. (2009) CPS and police strengthen approach to disability hate crime 23 January. www.communitycare.co.uk/Articles/2009/01/23/110524/cps-and-police-strengthen-approach-to-disability-hate-crime.htm

Scourfield, P. (2007) Social care and the modern citizen: client, consumer, service user, manager and entrepreneur. *British Journal of Social Work*, 37: 107–122

Secker, J., Hill, R., Villeneau, L. and Parkman, S. (2003) Promoting independence: but promoting what and how? *Ageing and Society*, 23, 2003: 375–391

Shakespeare, T. (2009) The cruel toll of disability hate crime. Guardian online 12/3/2010. www.guardian.co.uk/commentisfree/2010/mar/12/disability-hate-crime-david-askew

Sharkey, P. (1989) Social networks and social service workers. *British Journal of Social Work*, 19 (1): 387–406

Shipman, A. (1998) The pump that won't be primed. *The World Today*, 54 (12): 314–316

Short Report (1984) *Third Report from the Social Services Committee, Perinatal and Neonatal Mortality Follow up*. London: HMSO

Simanowitz, S. (1995) *Violence, harassment, and discrimination against disabled people in Great Britain*. Annual report for the European Disability Forum by Liberty

Sinclair, A. and Dickinson, E. (1998) *Effective Practice in Rehabilitation; The Evidence of Systematic Reviews*. London: King's Fund

Skerrett, D. (2000) Social work — a shifting paradigm. *Journal of Social Work Practice*, 14 (1): 63–73

Smale, G. et al. (1993) in Braye, S. and Preston-Shoot, M. (1995, p116) *Empowering Practice in Social Care*. Buckingham: Open University Press

Smith, G. (1989) Review. *Journal of Social Policy*, 18 (4): 264

Social Care Institute for Excellence (2005) *SCIE Research briefing 2: Access to primary care services for people with learning disabilities*. www.scie.org.uk/publications/briefings/briefing02/index.asp

Social Services Committee (1985) *Community Care. Second Report from the Social Services Committee, House of Commons*. HMSO: London

Spandler, H. (2004) Friend or foe? Towards a critical assessment of direct payments. *Critical Social Policy*, 24 (2): 187–209

SSI: Department of Health Social Services Inspectorate (1992) *Confronting Elder Abuse: In SSI London Region Survey*. London: HMSO

Stanley, N., Manthorpe, J. and Penhale, B. (eds) (1999) *Institutional Abuse, Perspectives across the life course*. London: Routledge

Steiner, A. (2001) Intermediate care: more than 'a nursing thing'. *Age and Ageing*, 30: 433–435

Stevenson, J. (2003) in Crouch, D. (2003, p20) Intermediary care, how nurses fit in. *Nursing Times*, 99: 31

Stevenson, O. (1996) *Elder Protection in the Community, What can we learn from child protection?* London: Crown Copyright

Stone, K.G. (1997) Awakening to Disability: Nothing About Us Without Us. Volcano, CA: Volcano Press

Swain, J., French, S., Barnes, C. and Thomas, C. (eds) (2004) *Disabling Barriers – Enabling environments* (2nd edn). London: Sage

Swantz, M. (1996) A personal position paper on participatory research: personal quest for living knowledge. *Qualitative Inquiry*, March, 2 (1): 120–137

Taylor, K. and Dodd, K. (2003) Knowledge and attitudes of staff towards adult protection. *Journal of Adult Protection*, 5 (4): 26–32

The Law Pages (2010) www.thelawpages.com/court-cases/print_sentence.php?id=3319 (accessed 1 February 2010)

Thompson, J. and Pickering, S. (2001) *Meeting The Health Needs of People Who Have a Learning Disability*. London: Ballière Tindall.

Thompson, N. (1993) *Anti-Discriminatory Practice*. London: Macmillan

Thompson, N. (1998a) Social work with adults, in R. Adams, L. Dominelli, and M. Payne (eds) *Social Work: Themes, Issues and Critical Debates*. Basingstoke: Palgrave

Thompson, N. (1998b) *Promoting Equality*. Basingstoke: Macmillan

Thompson, N. (2006) *Anti Discriminatory Practice* (4th edn). Basingstoke: Palgrave Macmillan

Thompson, N. and Thompson, S. (2001) Empowering older people: beyond the care model. *Journal of Social Work*, 1 (1): 61–76

Titmuss, R. (1968) *Commitment to Welfare*. New York: Pantheon Books

Titterton, M. (2005) *Risk and Risk Taking in Health and Social Welfare*. London: Jessica Kingsley

Tomlinson, C. (2006) An individual budget in practice. *Journal of Integrated Care*, 14 (1): 35–37

Twigg, J. (1989) Models of carers. *Journal of Social Policy*, 18 (1): 62–63

Twigg, J. (1997) Deconstructing the 'social bath': Help with bathing at home for older and disabled people. *Journal of Social Policy*, 26 (2): 211–232

Twigg, J. and Atkin, K. (1994) in Nolan, M. and Caldock, K. (1996, p80) Assessment: identifying the barriers to good practice. *Health and Social Care in the Community*, 4 (2): 77–85

Twigg, J. et al. (1990) *Carers and Services: A Review of Research*. London: HMSO

Ungerson, C. (1987) *Policy is Personal*. London: Tavistock

Ungerson, C. (1990) *Gender and Caring*. Hemel Hempstead: Harvester Wheatsheaf

Valios, N. and Ahmed, M. (2006) 'It makes life more ordinary'. *Community Care*, 2–8 November 2006, 26–27

Wade, S. and Lees, L. (2002) The who, why, what of intermediate care. *Journal of Community Nursing*, 16: 10

Wahler, J. and Gabbay, S.G. (1999) Gay male aging: a review of the literature. *Journal of Gay and Lesbian Social Services*, 6 (3): 1–20

Wall, R. (1990) Families and the community. *Social Science News*, 7

Walker, A. (1982) *Community Care*. Oxford: Blackwell and Robertson

Warburton, N. (1994) *Philosophy: The Basics* (3rd edn). London: Routledge

Ward, D. and Mullender, A. (1991) Empowerment and oppression: An indissoluble pairing for contemporary social work. *Critical Social Policy*, 11 (2): 21–29

Ward, R., River, L. and Fenge, L. (2008) Not hidden, silent or invisible: a comparison of two participative projects involving older lesbians and gay men in the UK. *Journal of Gay and Lesbian Social Services*, 20 (1/2): 147–165

Wardhaugh, J. and Wilding, P. (1993) Towards an explanation of the corruption of care. *Critical Social Policy*, 37: 4–31

Watson, D. (2007) The causes and manifestations of learning disability, Chapter 2 in Gates, B. (ed.) *Learning Disabilities: Towards Inclusion* (5th edn). Edinburgh: Churchill Livingstone/Elsevier

Webster, P. and Owen, G. (2003) Tories to scrap tuition fees. *The Times*, May 13:1

Wenger, G.C. (1990) in Jeffreys, M. (1990) *Growing Old in Twentieth Century Britain*. London: Routledge

Wienhardt, L.S., Bickham, N.L. and Carey, M.P. (1999) Sexual coercion among women living with severe and persistent mental illness: Review of the literature and recommendations for mental health providers. *Aggression and Violent Behaviour*, 4(3): 307–317

Williams, C. (1995) *Invisible Victims: Crime and abuse against people with learning disabilities*. London: Jessica Kingsley

Williams, F. (1992) in Biggs, S. (1993, p153) User participation and interprofessional collaboration in community care. *Journal of Interprofessional Care*, 7: 2

Williams, P. (2009) *Social Work with People with Learning Difficulties* (2nd edn). Exeter: Learning Matters

Williams, V., Simons, K., Gramlich, S., McBride, G., Snelham, N. and Myers, B. (2003) Playing the piper and calling the tune? The relationship between parents and direct payments for people with intellectual disabilities. *Journal of Applied Research in Intellectual Disabilities*, 16: 219–228

Wilmott, P. (1986) *Social Networks, Informal Care and Public Policy*. London: Policy Studies Institute

Wilmott, P. (1987) *Kinship in Urban Communities, Past and Present*. London: Policy Studies Institute

Wilton, T. (1997) *Good for You: A Handbook on Lesbian Health and Wellbeing*. London: Cassell

Wintour, P. (2004) Last-minute deal with Catholics averts rebellion on living wills. *The Guardian*, 15 December 2004, p15

Worcestershire County Council (2009) *How can I use my Individual Budget to get the support I need?* www.worcestershire.gov.uk

Young, I. (1990) *Justice and the Politics of Difference*. Princeton, NJ: Princeton University Press

Index

?